Push Notifications

by Tutorials

By Scott Grosch

Push Notifications by Tutorials

By Scott Grosch

Notice of Rights

Notice of Liability

Trademarks

ISBN: 978-1-950325-71-9

Table of Contents

Book License

By purchasing *Push Notifications by Tutorials*, you have the following license:

- You are allowed to use and/or modify the source code in *Push Notifications by Tutorials* in as many apps as you want, with no attribution required.
- You are allowed to use and/or modify all art, images and designs that are included in *Push Notifications by Tutorials* in as many apps as you want, but must include this attribution line somewhere inside your app: "Artwork/images/designs: from *Push Notifications by Tutorials*, available at www.raywenderlich.com."
- The source code included in *Push Notifications by Tutorials* is for your personal use only. You are NOT allowed to distribute or sell the source code in *Push Notifications by Tutorials* without prior authorization.
- This book is for your personal use only. You are NOT allowed to reproduce or transmit any part of this book by any means, electronic or mechanical, including photocopying, recording, etc. without previous authorization. You may not sell digital versions of this book or distribute them to friends, coworkers or students without prior authorization. They need to purchase their own copies.

All materials provided with this book are provided on an "as is" basis, without warranty of any kind, express or implied, including but not limited to the warranties of merchantability, fitness for a particular purpose and noninfringement. In no event shall the authors or copyright holders be liable for any claim, damages or other liability, whether in an action of contract, tort or otherwise, arising from, out of or in connection with the software or the use or other dealings in the software.

All trademarks and registered trademarks appearing in this guide are the properties of their respective owners.

Before You Begin

This section tells you a few things you need to know before you get started, such as what you'll need for hardware and software, where to find the project files for this book, and more.

What You Need

To follow along with this book, you'll need the following:

- **Xcode 13 and Swift 5**: Xcode is the main development tool for writing code in Swift. This book's content was tested with Xcode 13 and SwiftUI. You can download the latest version of Xcode for free from the Mac App Store.
- **Apple Developer Program membership**: While you can test local push notifications on the simulator, sending remote push notifications requires having the ability to build, sign and run your app on a **physical** device with a Push Notification certificate — a capability reserved for paid members of the Apple Developer Program. The Apple Developer Program annual fee is $99 USD, but the exact amount might change based on local currency. More information on these memberships can be found at https://developer.apple.com/programs/. The information in this book will still prove an invaluable reference and resource to a developer without a paid membership, though.

If you haven't installed the latest version of Xcode, be sure to do that before continuing with the book. The code covered in this book requires Swift 5 and Xcode 13 — you may get lost if you try to work with an older version.

The only two prerequisites for this book are an intermediate understanding of Swift and iOS development, along with a paid Apple Developer Program membership, if you wish to experiment with delivering remote notifications to devices.

Book Source Code & Forums

Where to Download the Materials for This Book

The materials for this book can be cloned or downloaded from the GitHub book materials repository:

- https://github.com/raywenderlich/not-materials/tree/editions/4.0

Forums

We've also set up an official forum for the book at https://forums.raywenderlich.com/c/books/push-notifications. This is a great place to ask questions about the book or to submit any errors you may find.

"This book is dedicated to my wife and daughter, both of whom gave up many a night so that I could work on it, as well as to my parents who always made sure a good education was a priority."

— *Scott Grosch*

About the Author

Scott Grosch is the author of this book. He has been involved with iOS app development since the first release of the public SDK from Apple. He mostly works with a small set of clients on a couple large apps. During the day, Scott is a Solutions Architect at a Fortune 500 company in the Pacific Northwest. At night, he's still working on figuring out how to be a good parent to a toddler with his wife.

About the Editor

Marin Bencevic is the tech editor of this book. He is a computer vision researcher and a Swift developer. He likes to work on cool iOS apps and games, nerd out about programming, learn new things and then blog about it. Mostly, though, he just causes SourceKit crashes. He also has a chubby cat.

Introduction

Push Notifications by Tutorials provides a beginner-to-expert path for developers who wish to learn everything there is about push notifications. This book teaches the basic building blocks of delivering push notifications, as well as how these notifications are constructed and delivered to your end user.

As you work through the book, you'll deliver basic push notifications and expand your knowledge from chapter to chapter — super-charging your notifications with additional abilities as you progress through the book: rich custom UI for notifications, custom actions, notifications with special triggers such as time or location and much more. You'll also learn how to build a Vapor-based web service to deliver your very own push notifications, without the need for a third-party provider.

This book uses the Swift language. If you want to brush up on your Swift knowledge before diving in, be sure to check out our classic Swift beginner books — Swift Apprentice (https://bit.ly/2XU2YdR) and UIKit Apprentice (https://bit.ly/3sE4Khb).

As always, we appreciate that the By Tutorials team is your resource for beginner and advanced development skills!

— The *Push Notifications by Tutorials* team

Section I: Push Notifications by Tutorials

Begin your journey into rich media notifications, notification actions, grouped notifications and more!

Chapter 1: Introduction

Push notifications are one of the most important interaction points of your app with your users. Simply put, a push notification is a way to send any type of data to your user's app, even if the user isn't actively using it. The user will normally see the push notification appear as a banner alert on the device, a badge on the app icon and/or a sound. Push notifications are a direct line of communication to your user. You can alert the user of new content, new messages from friends or any other interesting piece of information. Notifications also provide users with a quick way to interact with your app and allow for faster interaction via background data downloads.

Conversely, notifications can be a bane to app retention — meaning how likely a user is to continue using your app – if you send them too frequently or use them in a way that's not useful to your customers. For example, if you send notifications about app version upgrades or messages just telling them new content is available, that will lead to poor user experiences.

Push notifications may seem simple and straightforward at first because they aren't hard to use and almost everyone is familiar with them; however, knowing how and when to use them may prove challenging. With advancements over the years of various iOS releases bringing some exciting advanced features — such as Rich Media Notifications, Notification Actions, Grouped Notifications and more — you may quickly realize that you need a book to help you out. Well, here's that book!

In this book, you'll learn everything you need in order to create, send and receive push notifications, meaning notifications that come from an external service as opposed to locally from the device. You'll also cover how to handle local notifications because, sometimes, you don't need all the overhead of a remote notification; rather, it's enough to simply schedule a notification to appear at a specific point in the future or when you enter a specific location.

Once you've worked your way through this book, you'll be a master of push notifications and well on your way to implementing them inside your own apps!

However, as helpful as this book may be and as great as push notifications can be, it's critical that you always keep in mind that the user may never receive your notification. Not only can your users opt-out of them at any point in time, *there is no guarantee your push notifications will be delivered*. What this means, as a developer, is that you can't depend on push notifications for your app to function properly — but this doesn't mean your push notifications shouldn't be well-made and used responsibly, which is what will be covered in this book.

Getting Started

To follow along with the tutorials in this book, you'll need a Mac computer capable of running Xcode. You can get the latest version of Xcode for free from the Mac App Store (apple.co/1f2E3nY). While there are other platforms for developing iOS apps, none are officially supported by Apple and will not be covered in this book. This book is written with Xcode 13, iOS 15 and Swift 5.

Please note that you'll need a paid Apple Developer account in order to create a Push Notifications certificate and run any of the apps included in this book. While Apple's iOS Simulator is now capable of receiving push notifications during development, it is still not capable of receiving remote notifications. If you don't have a physical device, such as an iPhone or iPad, you won't be able to work through Chapter 6, "Server-Side Pushes".

You will also need an intermediate level of knowledge of Swift and iOS development. This book makes the assumption that you are already an experienced iOS developer and are looking for details on implementing push notifications in your apps, or looking for a great reference when working on your app's notifications.

If you need to brush up on your Swift or iOS skills, you may be interested in the following resources:

- *Swift Apprentice* (https://bit.ly/2XU2YdR)
- *UIKit Apprentice* (https://bit.ly/3sE4Khb)
- "Programming in Swift: Fundamentals" video tutorials (https://bit.ly/3kCNapj]
- "Your First iOS and SwiftUI App" video tutorials (https://bit.ly/35RnnFu)

Let's get started!

Chapter 2: Push Notifications

Push notifications are a useful feature that allow you to interact with your users outside of the normal flow of your app. A notification can be scheduled locally based on conditions such as time or location, or scheduled from a remote service and "pushed" to your device. Regardless of whether you are utilizing a local or remote notification, the general process for handling one is the same:

- Ask your user for permission to receive notifications.
- Optionally make changes to the message before display.
- Optionally add custom buttons for the user to interact with.
- Optionally configure a custom user interface to display the notification.
- Optionally take action based on what the user did with the notification.

What Are They Good For?

You'd be hard pressed in this day and age to *not* have seen a push notification at some point. They are capable of many actions:

- Displaying a message.
- Playing a sound.
- Updating the badge icon on your app.
- Showing an image or playing a movie.
- Giving the user a way to pick from a few options.
- Most anything that a `UIViewController` or `View` can implement.

While you can technically show any type of user interface as long as it fits within the bounds of a notification window, that doesn't mean you *should* do so. Always keep user experience in the forefront of your mind when designing a notification. Will your users want to see it, hear it or interact with it?

Remote Notifications

By far, the most common type of notification used is a **remote notification**, in which a cloud service, usually a web server, is utilized to tell Apple's servers that a notification should be built and sent to a device.

A remote notification can be a great fit for multiplayer games that are turn-based. Once an opponent has made his or her move, the user is sent a notification stating that it's now their turn. If the app has any type of data feed, such as a news app, then a silent remote notification can be used to proactively send data to the user's device so that the content is already there when they run the app the next time, versus having to wait for a network download.

Clearly, you don't want just anyone to be able to send messages to your users! Apple has built its **Apple Push Notification service** (APNs) using **Transport Layer Security** (TLS). TLS provides privacy and data integrity, which ensures that you, and only you, control your app's notifications.

Security

APNs utilizes cryptographic validation and authentication to ensure security of your messages.

Your server, called a **provider**, utilizes TLS to send notification requests to Apple, and the device uses an opaque `Data` instance — referred to as a **device token** — which contains a unique identifier that the APNs is able to decode. The iOS device receives a (possibly new) token when it authenticates with the APNs; the token is then sent to your provider so that a notification can be received in the future.

> **Note**: You should never cache a device token on the user's device as there are multiple instances in which APNs will need to generate a new token, such as installing the app on a new device or performing a restore from a backup.

The device token is now the **address** that a provider uses to reference a user's specific device. When the provider service wishes to send a notification, it will tell APNs the specific device token(s) that need to be sent a message. The device then receives the message and can take appropriate action based on the content of the notification. You can either build your own provider service, as discussed in Chapter 6, "Server-Side Pushes," or you can use one of the many third-party providers that already exist.

Notification Message Flow

It is important to understand the steps between registering your app with the Apple Push Notification Service and the user actually receiving a notification.

1. During `application(_:didFinishLaunchingWithOptions:)`, a request is sent to APNs for a device token via `registerForRemoteNotifications`.
2. APNs will return a device token to your app and call `application(_:didRegisterForRemoteNotificationsWithDeviceToken:)` or emit an error message to `application(_:didFailToRegisterForRemoteNotificationsWithError:)`.
3. The device sends the token to a provider in either binary or hexadecimal format. The provider will keep track of the token.

4. The provider sends a notification request, including one or more tokens, to APNs.
5. APNs sends a notification to each device for which a valid token was provided.

You can see these steps reflected in the image below:

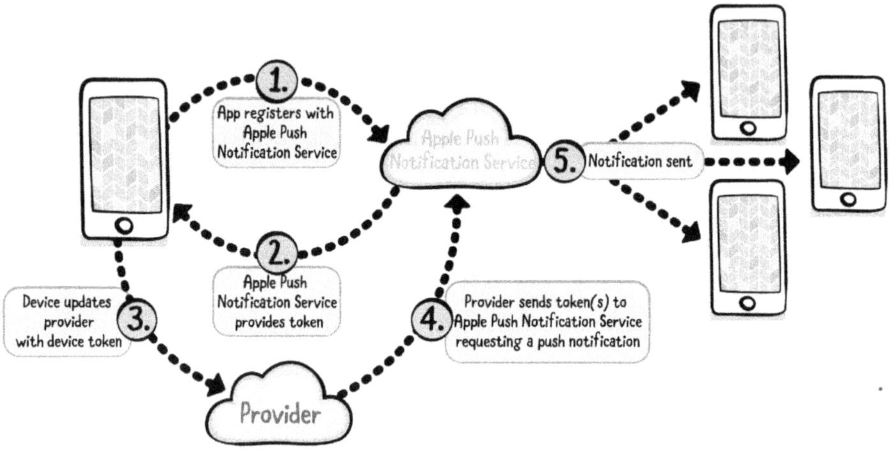

There are multiple ways a notification can materialize on a device once the notification has actually been pushed, depending on the state of the app and what features have been configured. Those will be discussed in greater detail in the chapters of this book.

Local Notifications

A **local notification** is created and scheduled on the device, as opposed to being sent to the device from a remote provider. A local notification allows all the same features as a remote notification. The only difference is that a local notification is triggered based on a set amount of time passing, or entering/exiting a geographical area, as opposed to being pushed to the device.

You might want to use a local notification similar to a timer. If your app teaches people how to cook in a step-by-step process, you may have a notification appear when the food has been marinating long enough and is now ready to go into the oven, with a new notification when it's time to take the food out of the oven.

Location-Aware Notifications

While it's easy to think of notifications as being in a type of sandbox of their own, there's no reason to exclude other iOS-provided features to enhance your app, such as location services. You can employ location services by tying a remote notification to a user's location. You may decide to send coupons to your customers, but only in a specific geographical area. Perhaps a guest author is reading at the local bookstore and you want to let your app's users know about it, but only if they live close enough to make it worthwhile.

Key Points

- Push notifications allow you to interact with your users outside of the normal flow of your app.
- A notification can be scheduled locally based on conditions or from a remote service and "pushed" to your device.
- **Remote notifications** are the most common type, and they use a Cloud service to determine that a notification should be built and sent to the device.
- Notification messages remain secure because APNs utilizes cryptographic validation and authentication.
- A **local notification** is created and scheduled on the device, as opposed to being sent to the device from a remote provider.

Where to Go From Here?

This chapter has been the first step in your journey to understanding the many facets, opportunities and challenges of leveraging push notifications.

Now that you know the basic terminology, it's time for you to actually learn how a notification request, known as a **payload**, is constructed.

Chapter 3: Remote Notification Payload

As you learned in Chapter 2, "Push Notifications," a remote **push** happens by sending data across the internet. That data is referred to as a **payload**, and it contains all of the information necessary to tell your app what to do when the push notification arrives. The cloud service is responsible for constructing that payload and sending it, along with one or more unique device tokens, to APNs.

Originally, notifications used a packed-binary interface, where each bit of the packet had a specific meaning. Using bitfields is much harder to handle and was confusing for many developers. Apple changed the payload structure and decided to use a single, simple, JSON structure. By using JSON, Apple ensured that the payload is simple to parse and construct in any language, while also providing the flexibility needed for the future, as new capabilities are added to push notifications.

There are a few keys in the JSON payload specifically defined by Apple, some of which are mandatory, but the rest of the keys and values are up to you to define as needed. This chapter will cover those predefined keys.

For regular remote notifications, the maximum payload size is currently 4KB (4,096 bytes). If your notification is too large, Apple will simply refuse it and you'll get an error from APNs. If you're suddenly worried that your push notifications won't work because you've got a sizable image to send, for example, don't worry! You'll learn how to download attachments in Chapter 10, "Modifying the Payload."

In this chapter, you'll learn how to construct the payload, what the various payload keys mean, how to supply custom data and how to handle collapsed and grouped notifications.

The aps Dictionary Key

The aforementioned JSON object is well-structured to hold all of the key pieces of data necessary to describe a push notification. The rest of this chapter will describe each key in detail.

The `aps` dictionary key is the main hub of the notification payload wherein everything defined and owned by Apple lives. Within the object at this key, you'll configure such items as:

- The message to be displayed to the end user.
- What the app badge number should be set to.
- What sound, if any, should be played when the notification arrives.
- Whether the notification happens without user interaction.
- Whether the notification triggers custom actions or user interfaces.

There are several keys you can use, each with their own considerations.

Setting the Alert

The key you'll use most often is the `alert` key. This key allows you to specify the message that will be displayed to your user. When push notifications were first released, the `alert` key simply took a string with the message. While you can, for legacy reasons, continue to set the value to a string, it's preferred that you instead use a dictionary. The most common payload for a message would include a simple `title` and `body`:

```
{
  "aps": {
    "alert": {
      "title": "Your food is done.",
      "body": "Be careful, it's really hot!"
    }
  }
}
```

Using a dictionary, instead of the legacy string, enables you to utilize both the title and body data points for your message. If you don't want a `title`, for example, simply leave that key/value pair out.

You may, however, run into some issues with this because of **localization**.

Localizing Notifications

Yes, the localization monster rears its ugly head, again! If the whole world could just agree on a single language, life would be so much simpler for us developers. You can quickly tell how using a dictionary isn't going to work for your non-English speaking users. There are two options to work around this issue:

1. Call `Locale.preferredLanguages` at registration and send the list of languages your user speaks to your server.

2. Store localized versions of all your notifications in your app bundle.

There are pros and cons to each approach, and it really depends on the quantity and type of notifications you'll be sending. If you keep everything on the server, and send each person the proper translation, you'll never have to push a new version of your app when you add new notification messages.

Conversely, that means more work on the server side and more customized push notification code versus just letting iOS handle the translations for you.

If you decide to handle localization on the app side, instead of passing along `title` and `body` keys, you can use `title-loc-key` and `title-loc-args` for the title, and `loc-key` and `loc-args` for the body.

For example, your payload might end up looking like this:

```
{
  "aps": {
    "alert": {
      "title-loc-key": "FOOD_ORDERED",
      "loc-key": "FOOD_PICKUP_TIME",
      "loc-args": ["2022-05-02T19:32:41Z"]
    }
  }
}
```

When iOS gets the notification, it'll look in the proper **Localizable.strings** file inside your app to automatically get the correct translation, and then substitute the date and time into the proper location. This might result in an English language speaker seeing:

```
You can pick up your order at 5:32 p.m.
```

Whereas a person reading Mandarin would see this instead:

```
你可以五點半領取
```

To keep the rest of the examples in this chapter simple, only the `title` and `body` keys will be used.

Grouping Notifications

Starting with iOS 12, adding the `thread-id` key to the `aps` dictionary will let iOS combine all notifications with the same identifier value into a single group in the notification center. Try to use a guaranteed unique value representing some thread of messages, such as the primary key from a database or a UUID.

```
{
  "aps": {
    "alert": {
      "title": "Your food is done.",
      "body": "Be careful, it's really hot!",
    },
    "thread-id": "casserole-12345"
  }
}
```

In a game app, you might use this feature so that all notifications related to a specific game session are grouped together and not merged in with all other game sessions. If you leave this key out, iOS will default to grouping everything from your app together into one group.

Keep in mind "grouping" notifications is different from "collapsing" notifications. Also, be aware that your users are able to turn off notification grouping in the iOS Settings app, if they so desire!

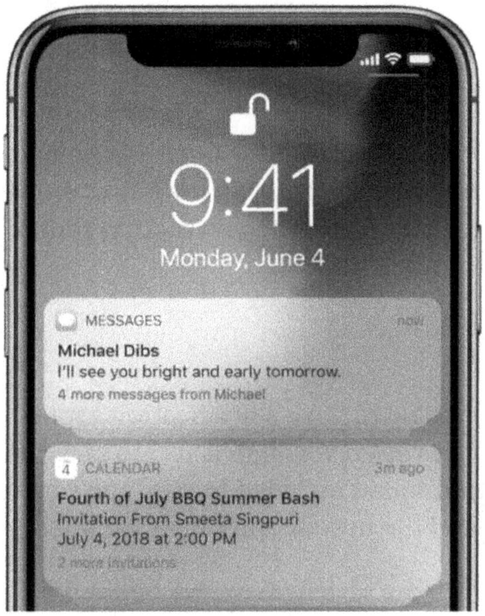

Adding a Badge

Since your users might not have had their phones handy when the alert message came through, you can also badge the app icon. The badge is the numeric value in a small red circle at the corner of the app icon on the home screen. If you'd like your app icon to display the numerical badge number, simply specify it using the `badge` key. To clear the badge and remove it, set the value to `0`.

> **Note**: The badge number is not a mathematical addition or subtraction. It's an absolute value that will be set on your app icon.

```
{
  "aps": {
    "alert": {
        "title": "Your food is done.",
        "body": "Be careful, it's really hot!"
    },
    "badge": 12
  }
}
```

What this means is that your server is going to have to know what number to display to the end user, which sometimes makes this key more trouble than it's worth. In Chapter 10, "Modifying the Payload," when we discuss service extensions, you'll learn a trick to work around this issue.

Adding Sound

When alerts arrive, it's possible to have a notification sound play. The most common value is simply the string `default`, which tells iOS to play the standard alert sound. If you want to use a custom sound included in your app's bundle, you can instead specify the name of a sound file in your app's main bundle.

Sounds must be 30 seconds or less. If they're any longer than 30 seconds, iOS will ignore your custom sound and fall back to the default sound.

> **Note**: Be very careful with custom or long sounds! It seems like a great idea when developing your app, but ask yourself this — will your end users appreciate your unique sound or the length of the sound? Be sure to do some user acceptance testing before deploying to the App Store.
>
> I had a client, for example, who provided a sports team management app. When a notification was delivered, it played the sound of a baseball being hit by a bat and the crowd roaring. Everybody thought it was pretty cool for about two days, and then he started getting bug reports begging him to remove it.

You can use the `afconvert` tool on your Mac to convert your custom sound to one of the four acceptable formats:

- Linear PCM
- MA4 (IMA/ADPCM)

- μLaw
- aLaw

For example, if you have an existing .mp3 file you would run a command like so:

```
afconvert -f caff -d LEI16 filename.mp3 filename.caf
```

Then, you can just add that new **filename.caf** to your Xcode project and include its name in your payload:

```
{
  "aps": {
    "alert": {
        "title": "Your food is done.",
        "body": "Be careful, it's really hot!"
    },
    "sound": "filename.caf"
  }
}
```

Critical Alert Sounds

If your app needs to display a critical alert, which will be discussed in Chapter 4, "Xcode Project Setup," you'll need to use a dictionary as the value of the `sound` key, instead of just a string:

```
{
  "aps": {
    "alert": {
        "title": "Your food is done.",
        "body": "Be careful, it's really hot!"
    },
    "badge": 12,
    "sound": {
      "critical": 1,
      "name": "filename.caf",
      "volume": 0.75
    }
  }
}
```

Notice the three keys used in the `sound` dictionary above:

- `critical`: Setting this to 1 will specify this sound is a critical alert.
- `name`: The sound file in the app's main bundle, as explained above.
- `volume`: A value between 0.0 (silent) and 1.0 (full volume).

Other Predefined Keys

Apple defines a few other keys as part of the aps dictionary, which will be discussed in greater detail in later chapters. These can be used for background update notifications, custom notification types, user interfaces and groupings of notifications.

Adding Custom Data

Everything outside of the aps key is for your personal use. You'll frequently find that you need to pass extra data to your app along with a push notification, and this is where you can do so. For example, if you're writing a geocaching app, you might want to send the user the next set of coordinates to investigate. You will, therefore, send a payload like so:

```
{
  "aps": {
    "alert": {
      "title": "Save The Princess!"
    }
  },
  "coords": {
    "latitude": 37.33182,
    "longitude": -122.03118
  }
}
```

In Chapter 8, "Handling Common Scenarios," you'll learn more about how to retrieve this data inside your app. As long as all of your custom data is kept outside of the aps dictionary, you'll never have to worry about conflicting with Apple.

Sending HTTP Headers

As discussed earlier, the payload is only one of a few things your server sends to APNs. Aside from a unique device token, you can send additional HTTP **header** fields to specify how Apple should handle your notification and how it is delivered to the user's device. It's unclear why Apple chose to place these as headers, instead of part of the payload.

Collapsing Notifications

One of those headers is the `apns-collapse-id` HTTP header field. Apple gives you the ability to collapse multiple notifications down to one when a newer notification supersedes an older one.

For example, if you're using a notification to alert users as to how many people have completed the scavenger hunt so far, you really only need to know the current total. While you're still diligently searching for that elusive item, three other people might have completed the game. Each time another person finds all their items, a push notification is sent to you. When you get the time to check on the status, you really don't want to see three separate notifications saying somebody has finished. Wouldn't you rather see a single notification saying three people are done? That's exactly what this header field is for.

You can put any unique identifier into the field, up to 64 bytes. When a notification is delivered, and this value is set, iOS will remove any other notification previously delivered that has the same value.

In the previous example of the scavenger hunt, it would make sense to use the unique ID from your database that represents that specific game. Shy away from using things like the name of the hunt to avoid inadvertently collapsing notifications that don't relate. Try to use guaranteed unique values instead. Any type of primary key from a database or a UUID are good examples of values to use.

> **Note**: If you're using a third-party delivery service, they'll have to provide a specific location for you to identify the `apns-collapse-id`. If this is a feature you think you'll utilize, be sure to look for it explicitly when you're shopping for a vendor.

Setting the Push Type

As of iOS 13 you are required to specify, in the headers, what type of push notification is being sent. You should specify a value of `alert` when the delivery of your notification displays an alert, plays a sound or updates the badge. For silent notifications that do not interact with the user you instead specify the value of `background`.

Apple's documentation states, "The value of this header must accurately reflect the contents of your notification's payload. If there is a mismatch, or if the header is missing on required systems, APNs may delay the delivery of the notification or drop it altogether."

Adding Priority

The third header you're likely to use is `apns-priority`. The default, if not specified, is 10. Specifying a priority of 10 will send the notification immediately, but is only appropriate for notifications which include an alert, sound or badge update.

Any notification which includes the `content-available` key **must** specify a priority of 5. Notifications with a priority of 5 might be batched and delivered together at a later point in time.

> **Note**: Apple's documentation states that it is an error to specify a priority of 10 for a notification whose payload contains the `content-available` key.

Key Points

In this chapter, you covered the basics of the remote notification payload. Some key things to remember:

- Prefer to use a dictionary instead of a string for the `alert` key.
- Consider how you're going to deal with localization issues: server-side vs. client-side.
- Utilize the `apns-collapse-id` HTTP header field when "overriding" or "updating" your notification is more appropriate than sending an additional notification.
- Place all of your custom data outside of the `aps` key to future-proof your custom keys.
- Think about whether grouping and/or collapsing your notifications makes sense.
- Ensure you are providing a value for the the new `apns-push-type` HTTP header.

Where to Go From Here?

If you want to learn more about notification payloads, you might be interested in reviewing Apple's documentation about Generating a Remote Notification (https://apple.co/2Ia9iUf). For information on sending notification requests to APNs, including other headers and status codes, refer to Apple's Sending Notification Requests to APNs (https://apple.co/2mn04ih) webpage.

With remote notification payloads covered, you're now ready to set up your app to receive notifications in Chapter 4, "Xcode Project Setup."

Chapter 4: Xcode Project Setup

Before you start sending and receiving push notifications, you first need to make sure your project is set up to do so!

In this chapter's materials you'll find a mostly default iOS app Xcode project in the **starter** folder. You'll set this project up to use push notifications. You could also create a brand new project by opening Xcode and creating a new **iOS App** project. Make sure to select **SwiftUI** as the **Interface** and leave the checkmarks at the bottom of the project creation screen unchecked.

In the Bad Ol' Days, this is the point in which you'd have to set up a custom profile with Apple to enable push notifications. Fortunately, with the current toolchains, this is all automated now.

Adding Capabilities

To tell Xcode that you'll be using push notifications in this project, just follow these four simple steps so that it can handle the registration for you:

1. Press ⌘ + 1 (or **View ▸ Navigators ▸ Project**) to open the **Project Navigator** and click on the top-most item (i.e. your project).
2. Select the **target**, *not* the project.
3. Open the **Signing & Capabilities** tab.
4. Click the + button.
5. Search for and select **Push Notifications** from the menu that pops up. If you don't see the Push Notifications capability, you're not using a paid Apple Developer account. Double-check that you selected the correct **Team** and check that you have a valid **Provisioning Profile** for your team and bundle ID.
6. Notice the **Push Notifications** capability added below your signing information.

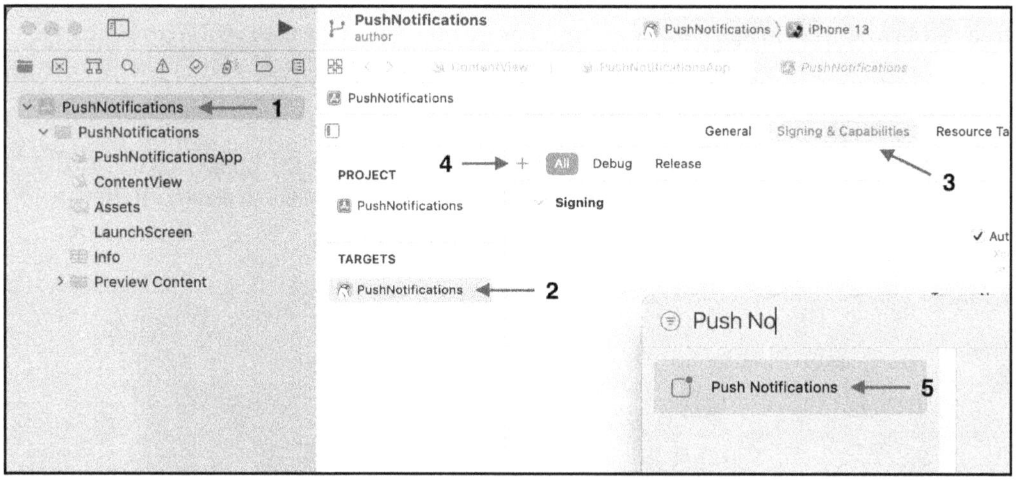

If you were to go back to the Member Center now and look at your provisioning profiles, you'd see that one has been generated specifically for this project with push notifications enabled. Well, that was so easy that it makes you wonder why Apple didn't make it this easy from day one!

Registering for Notifications

You've told Apple that you're going to use push notifications. Next, you'll have to add the required code to prepare your app for receiving push notifications. As push notifications are an opt-in feature, you'll have to request permissions from the user to enable them.

Because users can turn off notifications at any point, you need to check for whether or not they are enabled *every time* the app starts. The very first time, and only the very first time that your app requests access to push notifications, iOS will display an alert asking the user to accept or reject notifications. If the user accepts, or has previously accepted, you can tell your app to register for notifications.

Create a new Swift file called **AppDelegate.swift** and replace its contents with the following code:

```
import UIKit
import UserNotifications

class AppDelegate: NSObject, UIApplicationDelegate {
  // 1
  func application(
    _ application: UIApplication,
    didFinishLaunchingWithOptions launchOptions:
    [UIApplication.LaunchOptionsKey: Any]?
  ) -> Bool {
    // 2
    Task {
      let center = UNUserNotificationCenter.current()
      try await center.requestAuthorization(options:
[.badge, .sound, .alert])

      // 3
      await MainActor.run {
        application.registerForRemoteNotifications()
      }
    }

    return true
  }
}
```

SwiftUI projects no longer include an app delegate by default. Since you need the push registration code to run at every launch, you'll have to implement the delegate.

> **Note**: Even though you're using SwiftUI, the `UIApplicationDelegate` code comes from `UIKit`.

In the preceding code:

1. The `application(_:didFinishLaunchingWithOptions:)` method is where you should register for push notifications.
2. The delegate method is not yet async aware so you'll wrap the whole body in a new top-level task so you that can use the asynchronous version of the authorization call.
3. Once authorization checks are complete, you register for notifications back on the main thread.

If you're new to asynchronous programming with Swift, you may wish to read through our book, _Modern Concurrency in Swift (https://www.raywenderlich.com/books/modern-concurrency-in-swift)_.

Sharp readers may notice there's a `try` without any type of checks. An interesting side-effect of task blocks is that thrown exceptions are silently consumed and ignored.

Notice the addition of a new import statement to pull in the `UserNotifications` system framework. It's a bit hard to read due to the long length of the function name but, essentially, whenever the app starts, you request authorization from the user to send badges, sounds and alerts to the user. If any of those items are granted by the user, you register the app for notifications.

Since SwiftUI lifecycle apps no longer call the app delegate by default, you'll need to tell SwiftUI to use the app delegate you just created. Open **PushNotificationsApp.swift** and add these lines as the first statement in the `struct`:

```
@UIApplicationDelegateAdaptor(AppDelegate.self)
private var appDelegate
```

The above code uses the property wrapper syntax to tell Xcode that it should instantiate an instance of `AppDelegate`, which you just created, and then wire that up to the `appDelegate` property.

Build and run your app now. You'll see the request to allow notifications.

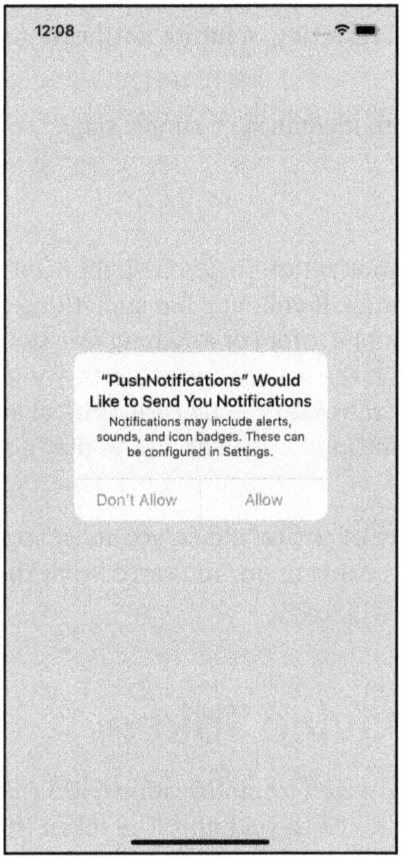

Since you're reading this book, you must want to see the notifications, so click on **Allow** in the alert.

Provisional Authorization

An alert like the one above can be somewhat jarring to a user when the app starts up the first time. Why are they being asked for this? What type of data are you going to send? If you talk to your friends and colleagues, you'll likely find that a surprising number of people, especially older people, simply reject all notifications.

To work around this issue, Apple provides another useful case for the `UNAuthorizationOptions` enum that you can pass to `requestAuthorization` during setup. If you include `.provisional` in the `options` argument, notifications will automatically be delivered silently to the user's Notification Center, without asking for permission – there will be no sound or alerts for these provisional notifications.

The benefit of this option is that users who look in Notification Center can see your notifications and decide if they're interested in them or not. If they are, they simply authorize them from there, resulting in future notifications appearing as regular push notifications.

That's quite a nice feature to include via a simple flag!

Critical Alerts

There's another type of authorization that you might need to request, depending on the type of app you're building. If your app has something to do with health and medicine, home security, public safety or anything else that may have the need to present a notification even if the user declined alerts, you can ask Apple to configure critical alerts via the `.criticalAlert` enum case. Critical alerts will bypass Do Not Disturb and ringer switch settings as well as always play a sound… even a custom sound.

Due to the disruptive nature of critical alerts, you must apply for a special entitlement from Apple to enable them. You can do that through the Apple Developer Portal (apple.co/2JwRvbv).

Getting the Device Token

If your app successfully registered for notifications, iOS will call another delegate method providing a device token to your app. The token is an opaque data type which is globally unique and identifies one app-device combination with the APNs.

Unfortunately, iOS provides this to you as a `Data` type instead of a `String`, so you'll have to convert it since most push service providers expect a string.

Add the following code to the end of `AppDelegate`:

```
func application(
  _ application: UIApplication,
  didRegisterForRemoteNotificationsWithDeviceToken deviceToken:
Data) {
  let token = deviceToken.reduce("") { $0 + String(format:
"%02x", $1) }
  print(token)
}
```

iOS will call this method once the device has successfully registered for push notifications. The token is a set of hex characters; the above code turns the token into a string of hexadecimal digits. There are multiple methods that you'll see on the internet for how to convert the `Data` type to a `String`. Use whatever method seems most natural to you, but keep in mind that some implementations you find online might be outdated. `reduce` is a method that combines the elements of a sequence into a single value using the given closure. So, in this case, you're simply taking each byte and converting it to hex, then appending it to the accumulated value.

> **Note**: Never make an assumption about the length of the token. Many tutorials you find will hardcode the length of a token for "efficiency". Apple has already increased the token length once before from 32 to 64 characters. When you store your device tokens in something like a SQL database, be sure to not hardcode a length or you may have issues in the future.
>
> Also, keep in mind that the device token itself can change. Apple will issue a new device token when the user installs the app on another device, restores from an old backup, reinstalls iOS and in some other cases. You should never try and link a token to a specific user.

Build and run the app **on a physical device**. You should see a device token (a string of random characters) in the Xcode console window:

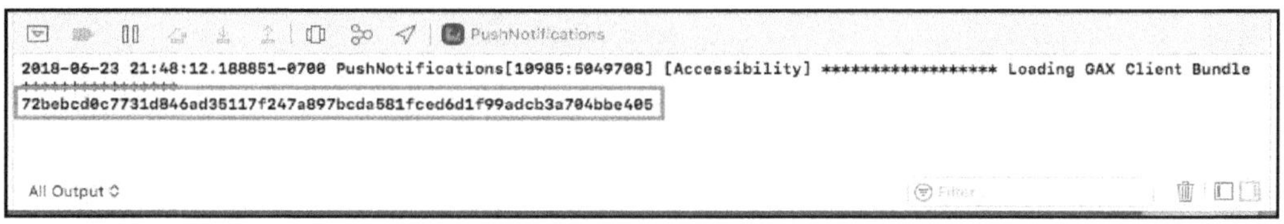

If you run on the simulator you won't see any output in the console. As the simulator is not able to receive notifications remotely, the delegate method is never called.

If you don't see the device token, it means that something went wrong during the setup process. To see what the problem is, add the following method to **AppDelegate.swift**:

```
func application(
  _ application: UIApplication,
  didFailToRegisterForRemoteNotificationsWithError error: Error)
{
  print(error)
}
```

iOS will call this method when it fails to register the device for pushes. You can now build and run again to check the error in your console.

Key Points

- You must tell Xcode that push notifications will be part of your project; follow the steps in this chapter so that Xcode can handle the registration for you.
- You must add the required code to prepare your app for receiving push notifications.
- Push notifications are an opt-in feature, so you must request permissions from the user to enable them.
- To avoid jarring notifications the first time a user opens an app, use **provisional authorization** so that notifications are delivered silently to the user's Notification Center, without asking for permission.
- For **critical alerts** that override a user's declined alerts, you must apply for a special entitlement from Apple to enable them, due to their disruptive nature.
- Once you have successfully registered your app for notifications, iOS will call a delegate method, providing a device token to your app. Never make assumptions about the length of your token or try to link the token to a specific user.
- Specify in your `App` struct implementation that you're using an app delegate.

Where to Go From Here?

At this point, you've technically done everything necessary to make your app capable of receiving and displaying a push notification. In the next chapter, you'll get your **Authentication Token** from Apple so that Apple's servers will allow you to send notifications and you'll finally send your first push notification!

For in-depth discussion of Apple's async/await implementation, check out Modern Concurrency in Swift (https://www.raywenderlich.com/books/modern-concurrency-in-swift).

Chapter 5: Sending Your First Push Notification

In the last chapter, you set up your app to be able to receive push notifications. The last piece that you'll need in order to have your app receive a push notification is an **Authentication Token** used by Apple's servers to trust your app. This token validates your server and makes sure that there's always a secure connection between your backend and APNs.

Authentication Token Types

When Apple first started allowing sending push notifications, it used the **PKCS #12** archive file format, also commonly known as the **PFX** format.

If you've ever worked with push notifications in the past, this file ends with the `.p12` file extension.

This type of format was quite cumbersome to work with for multiple reasons:

- They are only valid for a single year, requiring yearly "maintenance" of your certificates.
- You need separate certificates for both production and development distributions.
- You need separate certificates for every app you publish.
- Apple does not provide the certificate in the "final" format you'll actually need to send notifications, requiring you to run multiple `openssl` commands from Terminal for the multiple conversions; usually requiring a bit of research to remember how.

Around 2016, in order to work around the above problems, Apple started supporting the industry standard **RFC 7519**, better known as **JSON Web Tokens**, or JWT (https://jwt.io/). These tokens use the newer `.p8` file extension.

Apple, of course, likes its own names and so all of its documentation on push notifications refers to these as **Authentication Tokens**. Changing to the newer format alleviated all the issues of the **PFX** file format as they do not need to be renewed, don't differentiate between production and development, and can be used by **all** of your apps.

Unfortunately, Apple did very little other than say, "There it is!", when it released it. Unless you already had experience with HTTP/2 and JWT, you were stuck. We'll remedy that now!

Getting Your Authentication Token

Creating the Authentication Token is a simple process that you only have to do **once**. In a browser of your choice, go to the Member Center (https://apple.co/2HRPzxv), and sign in with your Apple ID.

1. In the side-bar, click on **Keys**.
2. Click on the blue "plus" button.

Once you click the plus button, the screen will change where you can enter your key's details.

1. Name the key **Push Notification Key**.
2. Enable the **Apple Push Notifications service (APNs)** checkbox.
3. Press **Continue**.

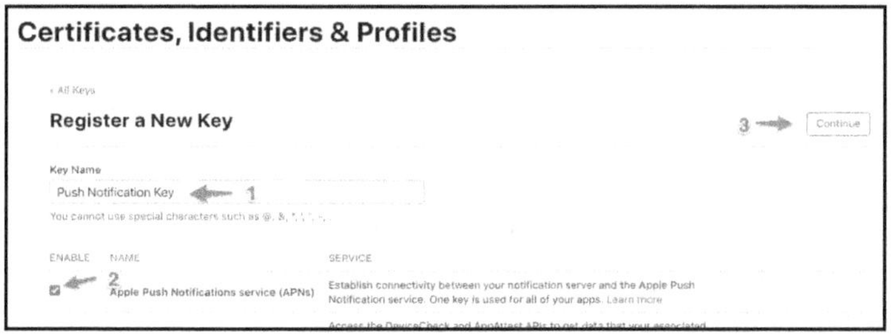

Now click **Register** on the screen that appears, then click **Download** and, finally, **Done**.

By default, the key will download to your **Downloads** directory and will be named something like **AuthKey_689R3WVN5F.p8**. The **689R3WVN5F** part is your **Key ID**, which you'll need when you're ready to send a push.

You'll also need to know your **Team ID**, so grab that now. At the very top-right of your browser window you'll see your Team ID listed right after your account name. It's a 10 character long string of letters and numbers.

Sending Push Notifications

At this point, you have everything you need to send a push notification to your app. You'll need some way to actually configure the push and send it manually.

Sending Push Notifications to the Simulator

While you should always test your push notifications against a physical device, during day-to-day development it'll be easier to test on the simulator so you don't have to continuously unlock your device.

Create a text file somewhere on your Mac named **payload.apns** which contains the notification you wish to send, such as the following:

```
{
  "aps": {
    "alert": "Hello"
  },
  "Simulator Target Bundle": "com.yourcompany.PushNotifications"
}
```

As you can see, the file is a standard JSON representation of a push notification with two differences. First, you've added the **Simulator Target Bundle** key, which should specify the name of your project's bundle identifier. Make sure to change that to match your project.

Second, you've used an **apns** extension on the filename. When you drag a file to the simulator with the apns extension, it knows that the file is a push notification payload, as opposed to a file to save.

Build and run the app from Chapter 4, "Xcode Project Setup," to a simulator. If you skipped Chapter 4 you can find the same project in this chapter's starter materials.

Once your app is running in the simulator, send it back to the home screen by selecting **Devices ▸ Home** (⇧ + ⌘ + H). Currently your app will not accept push notifications while running in the foreground. You'll fix that in Chapter 8, "Handling Common Scenarios".

Finally, open **Finder** on your Mac and drag the **payload.apns** file onto the simulator window. You should see your push notification.

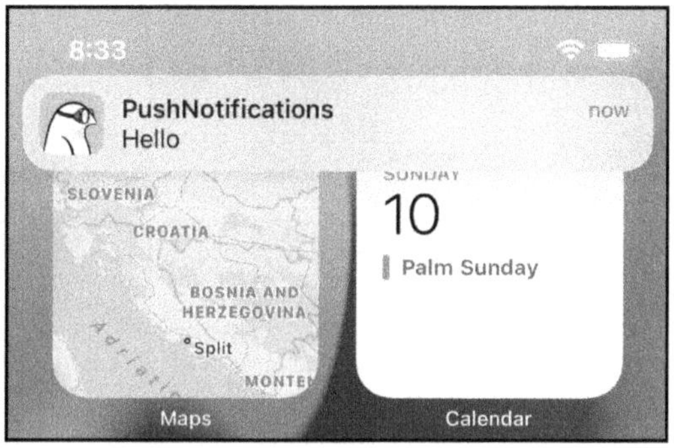

Sending Push Notifications to a Device

There are many free and open-source projects on GitHub which will allow you to send a push notification to your device; consider using PushNotifications (https://bit.ly/2jvEUtK) as it supports the newer Authentication Keys, which some of the other apps don't. You can use any of the apps out there as long as they support Authentication Keys.

Build and run the app from Chapter 4, "Xcode Project Setup," to a physical device. If you skipped chapter 4 you can find the same project in this chapter's starter materials.

Once the app has successfully launched, move the app to background, by either switching to your home screen or locking the device. With the way your notifications are configured right now, you'll only see them if you are *not* currently running the app in the foreground. You'll fix that later on in the book, in Chapter 8, "Handling Common Scenarios".

In your Xcode **console window** (⇧ + ⌘ + C), you'll see a long hex string printed out, which is the token from your `print` call during registration. Copy that string into your clipboard.

Now, launch the **PushNotifications** app you downloaded from GitHub (or any other similar tool). If using PushNotifications, you may need to right-click the app and then select **Open** to open in, to get around signing restrictions. You'll need to be sure to select the **TOKEN** authentication option and then select the p8 file you downloaded from the Developer Portal, and fill in your Key ID, Team ID, Bundle ID and Device Token.

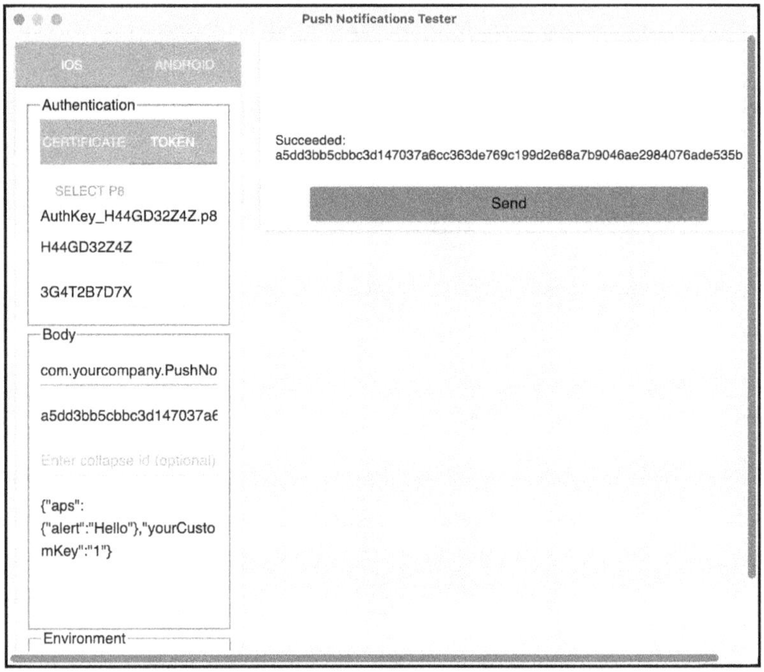

You don't need to change the payload at all. Once you press **Send**, you should see a notification appear on your device shortly thereafter!

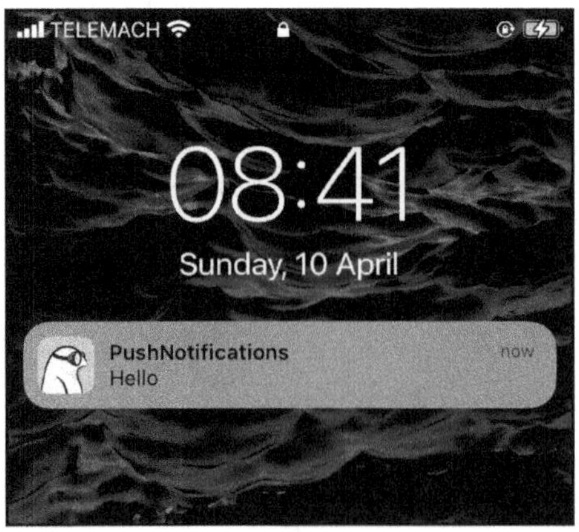

Key Points

- For your app to receive push notifications, you must have an **Authentication Token** used by Apple's servers to trust your app.
- The authentication token validates your server and makes sure that there's always a secure connection between your backend and APNs.
- Creating the Authentication Token is a simple process that you're only required to do once; follow the steps in the chapter to create yours.
- To configure the push and send it manually, there are many free and open-source projects on GitHub to provide this functionality — just make sure whatever you use supports Authentication Keys.
- If you're sending a push notification to the simulator, ensure the file has the **apns** extension and includes your bundle ID.

Chapter 6: Server-Side Pushes

While you've successfully sent yourself a notification, doing this manually won't be very useful. As customers run your app and register for receiving notifications, you'll need to somehow store their device tokens so that you can send them notifications at a later date.

Using Third-Party Services

There are a slew of services online that will handle the server-side for you. You can simply search Google for something along the lines of "Apple push notification companies" and you'll find multiple examples. Some of the most popular ones are:

- Amazon Simple Notification Service (SNS) (https://aws.amazon.com/sns/)
- Braze (https://bit.ly/2yM4hx7)
- Firebase Cloud Messaging (http://bit.ly/2Nq4b5x)
- Kumulos (https://bit.ly/2FIQ8Dy)
- OneSignal (https://bit.ly/1Ukk3WL)
- Airship (https://bit.ly/1QymqCY)

Each company will vary in its pricing and API, so discussing any specific service is beyond the scope of this book. If you want to get running quickly or don't want to deal with anything on the server-side, then solutions like the above may be perfect for you.

You may find, however, that you prefer avoiding third-party services, as you can run into issues if the service changes how its API works or if the company goes out of business. These services will usually also charge a fee based on how many notifications you send.

As an iOS developer, you might already be paying for a web hosting service for your website, which gives you the tools you need to do this work yourself — and you can find multiple vendors that charge $10 or less per month. Most web hosting services provide SSH access and the ability to run a database. Since handling the server-side only requires a single database table, a couple of REST endpoints, and a few easy-to-write pieces of code, you may want to do this work yourself.

If you have no interest in running your own server, you can skip to Chapter 7, "Expanding the Application."

> **Note**: Some examples in the rest of the book assume you are connecting to the server you'll set up in this chapter.

Installing Docker

If you don't already have Docker installed, please go to the Docker for Mac (https://dockr.ly/2JOzJ31) site and follow the installation instructions. Since you'll be using the Docker CLI tools, you might need to use the `docker login` command for the initial setup.

Generating the Vapor Project

Now it's time to build your web service. For this tutorial, you'll implement the web service with **Vapor**. Vapor is a very well supported implementation of server-side development using Swift. Without too much code you can use it to control your SQL database as well as your RESTful API. To use Vapor, though, there's a little bit of setup that needs to happen. If you're not familiar with Vapor, you can find a list of resources at the end of this chapter.

It's time to create your server app, which will allow you to store your web tokens!

If you had Vapor 3 or earlier installed on your machine, you'll need to remove the previous installation by running this command, in **Terminal**:

```
$ brew untap vapor/tap/vapor
```

If you don't have Vapor installed, or after removing the older version, run the following command in **Terminal**:

```
$ brew install vapor
```

> **Note**: If you don't have Homebrew already installed, install it by following the instructions at brew.sh.

Now, from **Terminal**, generate your project by running the following commands:

```
$ vapor new WebService --fluent.db Postgres --no-leaf
```

This sets up a new Vapor web service that uses the Posgres database. It already adds all the dependencies needed for Vapor and the database as well as a general folder structure with a few example files.

Next, navigate to the folder Vapor created for you.

```
$ cd WebService
```

The Vapor CLI has also generated appropriate Docker configuration files. Make sure you open **Docker** and give it the necessary permissions to install its helpers. Once Docker is running, from **Terminal**, tell Docker to bring your PostgreSQL database online:

```
$ docker-compose up db
```

If you're already running PostgreSQL natively on your Mac you'll get messages like this:

```
Recreating webservice_db_1 ...

Recreating webservice_db_1 ... error
```

```
ERROR: for webservice_db_1  Cannot start service db: driver failed
programming external connectivity on endpoint webservice_db_1
(388144b568ed26530852f351bb374db228e35ad5a246b26b53c5926f626b5fa6):
Bind for 0.0.0.0:5432 failed: port is already allocated
```

```
ERROR: for db  Cannot start service db: driver failed programming external
connectivity on endpoint webservice_db_1
(388144b568ed26530852f351bb374db228e35ad5a246b26b53c5926f626b5fa6):
Bind for 0.0.0.0:5432 failed: port is already allocated

ERROR: Encountered errors while bringing up the project.
```

Don't worry if that happens, the fix is quite simple! The last line of **docker-compose.yml** should be changed to this:

```
- '32768:5432'
```

That tells Docker to internally map port 5432, which is what PostgreSQL expects to use, to port 32768 on your Mac. By changing the port, you remove the conflict. UNIX defines ports 32768 – 65535 as available for your app to use.

When Docker successfully starts your database, you'll see output like this:

```
Recreating webservice_db_1 ... done
Attaching to webservice_db_1
db_1      |
db_1      | PostgreSQL Database directory appears to contain a database; Skipping initialization
db_1      |
db_1      | 2020-11-16 06:42:21.450 UTC [1] LOG:  starting PostgreSQL 12.3 on x86_64-pc-linux-musl, compiled by gcc (Alpine 9.3.0) 9.3.0, 64-bit
db_1      | 2020-11-16 06:42:21.450 UTC [1] LOG:  listening on IPv4 address "0.0.0.0", port 5432
db_1      | 2020-11-16 06:42:21.450 UTC [1] LOG:  listening on IPv6 address "::", port 5432
db_1      | 2020-11-16 06:42:21.455 UTC [1] LOG:  listening on Unix socket "/var/run/postgresql/.s.PGSQL.5432"
db_1      | 2020-11-16 06:42:21.509 UTC [20] LOG:  database system was shut down at 2020-11-02 00:26:24 UTC
db_1      | 2020-11-16 06:42:21.522 UTC [1] LOG:  database system is ready to accept connections
```

Adding Support for Tokens

In **Finder**, navigate to your **WebService** folder and double-click on the **Package.swift** file.

Vapor uses Apple's **Swift Package Manager** to generate the Xcode project. Instead of opening an Xcode project file, you open the **Package.swift** file with Xcode. After opening it, Xcode will take a few minutes to fetch all of your project's dependencies. You'll know it's done downloading the dependencies when Xcode shows the version number next to each listed package.

Defining the model

The device token you receive from Apple is the *model* that you'll store. Create the **Sources/App/Models/Token.swift** file and add the following code into it:

```
import Fluent
import Vapor

final class Token: Model {
  // 1
  static let schema = "tokens"

  // 2
  @ID(key: .id)
  var id: UUID?

  // 3
  @Field(key: "token")
  var token: String

  @Field(key: "debug")
  var debug: Bool

  // 4
  init() { }

  init(token: String, debug: Bool) {
    self.token = token
    self.debug = debug
  }
}
```

Vapor's `Model` is how you represent a table in the database. All of the models you create will follow the above template.

1. You identify what the name of the table is in the database.
2. You identify what the primary key is. Vapor **requires** the Swift variable for the identifier to be called `id`. You can use almost any type but the convention for Vapor is that the ID should be a `UUID` as that's portable to all database types.
3. Next, you'll create a property for each column in the database. Using the `@Field(key:)` property wrapper, you tell Swift what the name of the column is in the database. In the examples above, the SQL column name matches the Swift variable. However, if the database uses snake_case, you'll be able to map back to a camelCase Swift variable.

4. Finally, you create the required initializers. A Vapor model always requires an empty initializer, and you'll generally want to provide one that takes the non-ID properties.

When you're creating a new token, you'll not have an ID to specify, which is why that has to be specified as an optional value.

Configuring the Database Table

Now Xcode knows the structure of your model, but it doesn't yet exist in the database. Vapor will handle that task for you as well!

Create the file **Sources/App/Migrations/CreateToken.swift** and paste the following code:

```
import Vapor
import Fluent

struct CreateToken: AsyncMigration {
  func prepare(on database: Database) async throws {
    try await database.schema(Token.schema)
      .id()
      .field("token", .string, .required)
      .field("debug", .bool, .required)
      .unique(on: "token")
      .create()
  }

  func revert(on database: Database) async throws {
    try await database.schema(Token.schema).delete()
  }
}
```

Vapor uses a process called **migrations** to handle the creation and deletion of database tables, which is implemented via the `Migration` protocol

The `Migration` code is what Vapor uses to properly create the database schema. This simply tells PostgreSQL to create the table if it doesn't already exist, make a required column for each property in the `Token` class, then ensure that the `token` column has a `UNIQUE` constraint assigned to it.

Creating the Controller

Now that you've got a model, you'll need to create the controller that will respond to your HTTP `POST` and `DELETE` requests. Controllers in Vapor are similar to a `UIViewController` in Swift. They are what *controls* the implementation.

You will need to create a couple of endpoints for your HTTP clients to call.

Creating Tokens

Create the **Sources/App/Controllers/TokenController.swift** file and add the following code:

```
import Fluent
import Vapor

struct TokenController {
  func create(req: Request) async throws -> HTTPStatus {
    // 1
    let token = try req.content.decode(Token.self)
    // 2
    try await token.create(on: req.db)
    // 3
    return .created
  }
}
```

The `create(req:)` method is where you implement the creation of a new database token in the database. While there are only three lines of code, there's quite a bit of functionality!

1. First, the method examines the content of the request and attempts to decode the JSON payload into the `Token` structure which you previously defined. If the payload doesn't match the structure then the method will throw an error.
2. Once the content has been decoded, the data is created as a new row in the database.
3. Returning `.created` generates a 201 status code, letting the caller know their object was created. You could also return an HTTP status code of `.noContent`, which equates to a 204 status.

Database operations are slow and expensive, which is why the methods are defined asynchronously.

Deleting Tokens

Now that you have a way to create tokens, you should probably handle the need to delete tokens which are no longer valid. Add this method to your controller:

```
func delete(req: Request) async throws -> HTTPStatus {
  // 1
  guard let token = req.parameters.get("token") else {
    return .badRequest
  }

  // 2
  guard let row = try await Token.query(on: req.db)
    // 3
    .filter(\.$token == token)
    // 4
    .first()
  else {
    // 5
    return .notFound
  }

  // 6
  try await row.delete(on: req.db)
  // 7
  return .noContent
}
```

The nice thing about the Vapor framework is that it's pretty intuitive to figure out what is happening. Even if you're completely new to Vapor, I bet you can figure out what the code is doing.

1. Start by grabbing the **token** parameter from the request. If the caller didn't provide a token, return a `.badRequest` call, which is an HTTP status 400.
2. You've identified that you want to search the database's `Token` table.
3. Instead of querying every token, filter the results to just the token you asked for. Notice how Vapor uses Swift 5's property wrappers. It's easy to forget to add that '$' to the keypath!
4. SQL queries can always return multiple rows. However, since you made the token a unique constraint in the database, you can tell Xcode to just grab the first record.
5. If no rows were returned, then send the client a `.notFound` status, which is HTTP status code 404. Some people prefer to send a `.badRequest` instead.

6. Now that you've identified the row in the database, delete it.
7. It's good practice to return `.noContent`, HTTP status code 204, when a method succeeds but there's nothing to tell the caller other than that.

Pay attention to the fact you've done the lookup via the token and *not* the token's database ID. You'll only try to delete a token if Apple said that the token was invalid. When that happens, the calling client has no idea what the primary key is in your database. It just wants to pass the token itself.

Setting up Routes

In the `delete` method you just implemented, you're expecting the caller to pass the token which should be deleted as part of the request. When the calling HTTP client connects to a URL like this:

```
https://..../token/0549f2c6d0d2887b0f8122b8b1ac45
```

You want it to call your `delete` method and know that the `token` parameter is the `0549f2c6d0d2887b0f8122b8b1ac45` part.

To accomplish linking a URL to a method, you'll set up what is known as routing. Add the following code to the end of the file:

```
extension TokenController: RouteCollection {
  func boot(routes: RoutesBuilder) throws {
    let tokens = routes.grouped("token")
    tokens.post(use: create)
    tokens.delete(":token", use: delete)
  }
}
```

At startup, when properly registered, the `boot(routes:)` method will be called to register the aforementioned routes. By calling `routes.grouped("token")` you're letting Vapor know that you'll be implementing a group of routes that are all accessible after the `token` component of a URL.

Then you've identified that when making an HTTP `POST` request, the `create` method defined on `TokenController` should be executed.

Similarly, you've identified that when an HTTP `DELETE` request is sent that it should call the `delete` method on `TokenController`. However, this time, you've specified that after the `tokens` part of the URL you'll provide one more path component. That last piece will be assigned to the **token** parameter which you queried at the start of the `delete(req:)` method. Placing the `:` character at the start of the string lets Vapor know you're identifying a placeholder, as opposed to wanting the text `token` to appear in the URL.

There's just one last piece to making your two routes work. Remember how I said, "When properly registered"? Open **Sources/App/routes.swift** and you'll see the default example that Vapor provided when you created the project. Delete the entire implementation of the `routes(_:)` method and replace it with a single line:

```
try app.register(collection: TokenController())
```

Registering a collection is how you identify that the controller has implemented the `RouteCollection` protocol.

That's all you need for handling APNs tokens! You might be wondering why there are no methods to *get* a token. If you consider the usage of the API, you need to store and delete tokens. There's never a case in which you would want an HTTP client to be able to find out which APNs tokens are registered.

Configuring the App

Because you're running the server locally during debugging, you'll have to take an extra step to tell Vapor that it should respond to more than just local connections. You *only* have to do this during development.

Edit the file **Sources/App/configure.swift** and add the following lines just before the `// register routes` comment.

```
if app.environment != .production {
  app.http.server.configuration.hostname = "0.0.0.0"
}
```

By setting the hostname to `0.0.0.0` you've let Vapor, and your Mac, know that it should accept HTTP connections that come from outside the Mac. When your iOS app starts up and wants to register with your web service for push notifications, it has to be allowed to connect over WiFi.

Registering the Migrations

There's just one step left to make everything work. You have to tell Vapor that it should run the migrations for the `Token` class. While still in **configure.swift**, replace this line:

```
app.migrations.add(CreateTodo())
```

with these lines:

```
app.migrations.add(CreateToken())
try! app.autoMigrate().wait()
```

The todo files are provided as samples, so there's no reason to register a migration for it. Vapor will not regenerate your database tables based on the migrations you define automatically unless you tell it to.

Build and run your project. If you're getting error messages related to NIO, that usually means there's a problem connecting to your database. Some common items you may want to look into if you get errors:

1. Is another webserver running on port 8080? Try `lsof -i :8080`.
2. Is another Docker instance already running?

- Use `docker ps` to find your container, and then stop it with `docker stop <container-id>`, and re-run the docker setup command from earlier in this chapter.

3. Are the database, user and password all configured correctly?

Testing Your API

At this point, you can use any REST-capable app to test out your endpoints. As a developer, you're likely already familiar with the **curl** command. Open a **Terminal** window and enter the following:

```
curl -i -X POST -H 'Content-Type: application/json' \
  -d '{"debug": true, "token": "xyz"}' localhost:8080/token
```

You should see **HTTP/1.1 201 Created** in the response body, telling you that your token was stored in the database and given a unique identifier.

Running Your iOS App

Now that your server is operational and has an endpoint to store a token, you can make your iOS app send the token to the server once it registers for push notifications. Chapter 7, "Expanding the Application" already includes a ready-made app that performs this task in the **final** folder of its materials. With your Vapor application still running, open the **PushNotfications** iOS app from Chapter 7's ***final*** materials in a separate Xcode window.

You'll need to know the IP address of your Mac so that your iOS app can make a connection to the webserver. It's relatively easy to find the IP address by clicking on the Apple icon in your Mac's menu bar and then choosing the **System Preferences...** option.

In the search field, simply type **ipv4** and select the `IPv4` item shown in the drop-down:

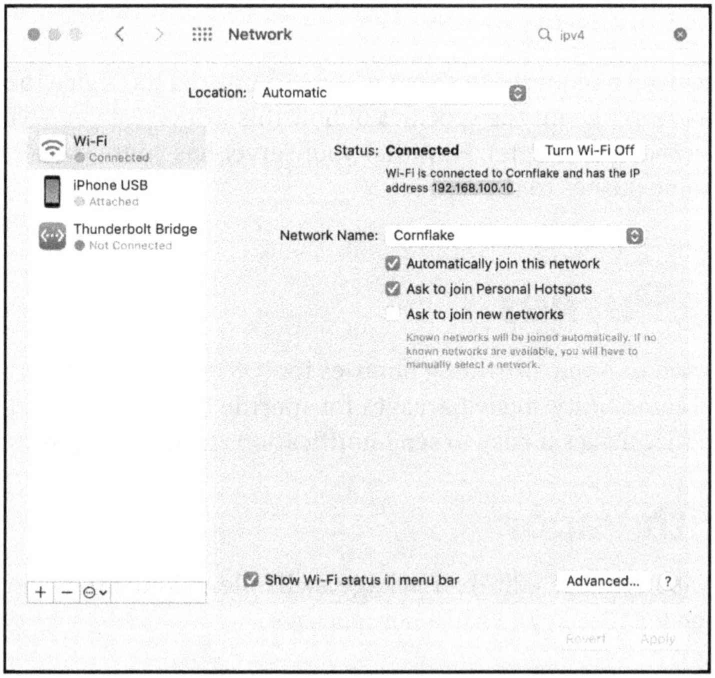

> **Note**: This is your internal IP address, not what's visible outside your network. Do not try to use a webpage like www.whatsmyip.org to get this value!

Open **AppDelegate.swift** and change the IP address in the `PushNotifications.send(token:to:)` call to the one from System Preferences. It should look like `http://YOUR-IP-ADDRESS:8080/token`. Finally, build and run the iOS project on a device.

> **Note**: If you don't see the `PushNotifications.send(token:to:)` call, you opened the starter project, instead of the final project.

When the device runs, you should see the details that are sent to your server in Xcode's console window. For example:

```
{
  "token" :
"74bbbd678ccc82021ea59a4681d702d48fbc415ea87f99ac721fdebc30716ff
7",
  "debug" : true
}
```

Your server received a request from your device and stored its device token in the database. Don't worry about the specifics of how this works just yet — you'll go over the iOS code in the next chapter. Now that your server has your device's token, it's time to send some pushes to the device!

Sending Pushes

While you're used to Apple providing libraries for iOS development, server-side Swift is built around community-made packages for specific tasks. Vapor has their own APNs package that makes it easy to send notifications through Apple's servers.

Send With Vapor

Back in your Vapor project, edit the **Package.swift** file. Add the following line to the top-most `dependencies` key to add a new package:

```
.package(url: "https://github.com/vapor/apns", from: "2.0.0")
```

Next, under the `targets` key, add the following line inside `dependencies` to add the new package's corresponding product:

```
.product(name: "APNS", package: "apns")
```

Don't forget to add a comma after the previous item. After closing **Package.swift**, Xcode will download the package, as well as its dependencies, and show them in the navigator with all the other Swift Package Dependencies.

The first step is to configure Vapor with APNs, so edit **configure.swift** to add the appropriate import:

```
import APNS
```

Then, add the following code at the end of the `configure(_:)` method:

```
let apnsEnvironment: APNSwiftConfiguration.Environment
apnsEnvironment = app.environment == .production ? .production :
.sandbox

let auth: APNSwiftConfiguration.AuthenticationMethod = try .jwt(
  key: .private(filePath: "/full/path/to/AuthKey_...p8"),
  keyIdentifier: "...",
  teamIdentifier: "..."
)

app.apns.configuration = .init(
  authenticationMethod: auth,
  topic: "com.yourcompany.PushNotifications",
  environment: apnsEnvironment)
```

There are a couple of things that you need to modify to match your project:

1. Change the key's `filePath` to be a path to the your .p8 authentication key file you obtained in the previous chapter. Be sure that you specify a fully qualified path!

2. `keyIdentifier` is the middle part of the filename that you downloaded from Apple. If you didn't rename the file, just strip off the **AuthKey_** prefix and the **.p8** suffix from the filename.

3. `teamIdentifier` comes from your developer account's Membership page (https://apple.co/2tXpJ2m).

4. Finally, make sure to change the `configuration`'s `topic` to match your apps bundle ID.

Edit the **TokenController.swift** file and import the APNS module:

```
import APNS
```

Now add a new method to the end of the struct to send everyone in the database a notification.

```
func notify(req: Request) async throws -> HTTPStatus {
  let tokens = try await Token.query(on: req.db).all()

  guard !tokens.isEmpty else {
    return .noContent
  }
}
```

It'd be rare you send everyone in the database a push notification, but for this example, since you're the only registered user, it works for the example. You're simply grabbing all tokens, returning `.noContent` if there aren't any registered tokens.

Next, create the alert that you wish to send. The `APNSwiftAlert` class has multiple constructors with a ton of options. Be sure to check out the various options available. Add the following line to the end of the function:

```
let alert = APNSwiftAlert(title: "Hello!", body: "How are you
today?")
```

Finally, you'll want to loop through each token and actually send the message.

> **Note**: At the time of writing, Vapor's APNs support does not natively support Swift's new asynchronous methods. Be sure to check the documentation when using this example as it has probably been implemented by now.

As Vapor's APNs package is still using futures for asynchronous operations, you'll need to wrap the code in a `withCheckedThrowingContinuation`. That's Swift's way of allowing you to wrap a non-`async` call in an `async` method. Usually you'd use it for a synchronous operation which you want to make asynchronous, but it works to handle futures as well.

```
  // 1
  return try await withCheckedThrowingContinuation
{ continuation in
    do {
      try tokens.map { token in
```

```
        // 2
        req.apns.send(alert, to: token.token)
          // 3
          .flatMapError {
            // 4
            guard
              case let
APNSwiftError.ResponseError.badRequest(response) = $0,
              response == .badDeviceToken
            else {
              // 5
              return req.db.eventLoop.future()
            }

            // 6
            return token.delete(on: req.db)
          }
      }
      // 7
      .flatten(on: req.eventLoop)
      .wait()
    } catch {
      // 8
      continuation.resume(throwing: error)
    }

    // 9
    continuation.resume(returning: .noContent)
  }
```

The preceding code works as follows:

1. You setup a *continuation* operation to wrap the code into an `async` aware code block.
2. Send the alert to the specified token, using the request's `apns` property.
3. Calling `flatMapError` unwraps the future returned from `send(_:to:)` on failure.
4. If APNs returns an error, check to see if it's a `.badDeviceToken`.
5. If it's not a `.badDeviceToken` then simply ignore the error. The code shown is how Vapor passes back an empty future.
6. If it was a `.badDeviceToken`, remove it from the database so that you don't try to send more notices to that device.
7. The `flatten(on:)` method compresses all the futures together and then you `wait()` for them to complete.

8. If there was an error, then pass it to the continuation block, which causes the error to be thrown again in the proper context.
9. Finally, if there were no exceptions, then tell the method to return a `.noContent` HTTP status code.

You can see how painful futures are to work with. Once the APNs library supports native Swift asynchronous operations, the above code will be something more like this:

```
for token in tokens {
  do {
    try await req.apns.send(alert, to: token.token)
  } catch {
    if let APNSwiftError.ResponseError.badRequest(response) =
error, response == .badDevice {
      try? await token.delete(on: req.db)
    }
  }
}

return .noContent
```

In order to be able to call that route, add another line to the end of the `boot(routes:)` method:

```
tokens.post("notify", use: notify)
```

Build and run the web service again, and then send a POST to the new route. With curl, send the following command:

```
curl -X POST localhost:8080/token/notify
```

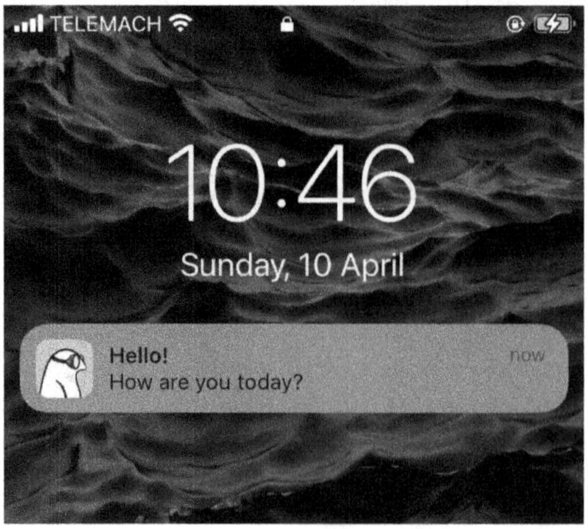

If everything worked, your device should receive a push notification! While the sample app sends notifications based on a route, you wouldn't normally do that in a production app. Using a route is just an easy way to show you the code necessary to send a push notification.

Send With curl and PHP

Before it was possible to use Swift, PHP with `libcurl` was the most common solution used by developers to send a push notification. If you wish to use PHP, you'll need to make sure that the `curl` command built for your system supports HTTP2. Run it with the `-V` flag and ensure you see **HTTP2** in the output:

```
$ curl -V
curl 7.48.0 (x86_64-pc-linux-gnu) libcurl/7.48.0 OpenSSL/1.0.2h
zlib/1.2.7 libidn/1.28 libssh2/1.4.3 nghttp2/1.11.1
Protocols: dict file ftp ftps gopher http https imap imaps ldap
ldaps pop3 pop3s rtsp scp sftp smb smbs smtp smtps telnet tftp
Features: IDN IPv6 Largefile NTLM NTLM_WB SSL libz TLS-SRP
**HTTP2** UnixSockets
```

If `HTTP2` isn't there, you'll need to install a newer version. If your target system supports Homebrew (https://brew.sh) then you can install by running these commands:

```
$ brew install curl-openssl
$ echo 'export PATH="/usr/local/opt/curl/bin:$PATH"' >> ~/.zshrc
```

Once you do that, restart Terminal and run `curl -V` again. You should now see `HTTP2` in the list of features.

If you're using some type of Linux system, you'll have to build curl yourself. That can become quite cumbersome though as you'll also need nghttp2, openssl, etc...

On to the script! Create a new file using your favorite editor called **sendPushes.php**. This isn't part of your Xcode project so store it wherever you're keeping your webserver's source files. You'll create a small PHP script that will send a HTTP/2 network request to APNs.

Firstly, you'll need to specify your Auth Key details and what the payload will be:

```
<?php

const AUTH_KEY_PATH = '/full/path/to/AuthKey_keyid.p8';
const AUTH_KEY_ID = '<your auth key id here>';
const TEAM_ID = '<your team id here>';
const BUNDLE_ID = 'com.yourcompany.PushNotifications';
```

```
$payload = [
  'aps' => [
    'alert' => [
      'title' => 'Hello!',
      'body' => 'How are you today?',
    ],
    'sound'=> 'default',
  ],
];
```

Fill in those `const` values based on your specific details.

Next, create a method to get your list of tokens. This will be very app-specific, but as a simple example, you can just get all the registered tokens in the database.

Add the following code below your `$payload` variable:

```
$db = new
PDO('pgsql:host=localhost;dbname=apns;user=apns;password=passwor
d');

function tokensToReceiveNotification($debug) {
  $sql = 'SELECT DISTINCT token FROM tokens WHERE debug
= :debug';
  $stmt = $GLOBALS['db']->prepare($sql);
  $stmt->execute(['debug' => $debug ? 't' : 'f']);

  return $stmt->fetchAll(PDO::FETCH_COLUMN, 0);
}
```

Notice how you're differentiating between debug and production tokens.

> **Note**: Any app that was installed directly via Xcode is considered a debugging app and must be sent to a different server than apps installed via TestFlight or the App Store. More on this in a moment.

The only tricky part to sending a push notification using the newer HTTP/2 protocol is getting the authentication header right. This is the part that Apple didn't provide much guidance on when it released its authentication token implementation.

Append the following code:

```
function generateAuthenticationHeader() {
  // 1
  $header = base64_encode(json_encode([
                 'alg' => 'ES256',
```

```
                'kid' => AUTH_KEY_ID
            ]));

    // 2
    $claims = base64_encode(json_encode([
                'iss' => TEAM_ID,
                'iat' => time()
            ]));

    // 3
    $pkey = openssl_pkey_get_private('file://' . AUTH_KEY_PATH);
    openssl_sign("$header.$claims", $signature, $pkey, 'sha256');

    // 4
    $signed = base64_encode($signature);

    // 5
    return "$header.$claims.$signed";
}
```

The preceding code takes care of generating the needed JWT authentication header. Breaking it down:

1. You specify that the encryption algorithm (`alg`) is using the SHA-256 hash algorithm and that the key identifier (`kid`) is the 10-character identifier from your p8 file.
2. Next, you'll generate the claims payload by specifying the issuer (`iss`) using your 10-character Team ID, obtained from your developer account (https://apple.co/2tXpJ2m), along with the issue time (`iat`), when the JWT was generated, in terms of the number of seconds since the epoch, in UTC.
3. You read your p8 auth key file and digitally sign the header and claim into `$signature`.
4. You take your digitally signed `$signature` and encode it using base 64.
5. Finally, you wrap it up by concatenating all three pieces, which you'll pass down to the `Authentication` header.

The only signature algorithm that Apple accepts is the ES256 algorithm. Don't try to sign the payload with any other algorithm or Apple will send an `InvalidProviderToken (403)` response to your request.

You should generate a new authentication header at the start of every group of pushes that you'll be sending. Additionally, these generated tokens last for about an hour; any request sent with a token older than an hour will be rejected by Apple with a `ExpiredProviderToken (403)` error.

You'll notice that nothing here actually encrypts the header. JWTs are signed and encoded, but they do nothing to provide security for sensitive data.

Now that you know what tokens you need to send and how to sign your request, you'll open an HTTP/2 session to the APNs. Add the following function to the file:

```
function sendNotifications($debug) {
  $ch = curl_init();
  curl_setopt($ch, CURLOPT_HTTP_VERSION, CURL_HTTP_VERSION_2_0);
  curl_setopt($ch, CURLOPT_POSTFIELDS,
json_encode($GLOBALS['payload']));
  curl_setopt($ch, CURLOPT_RETURNTRANSFER, true);
  curl_setopt($ch, CURLOPT_HTTPHEADER, [
      'apns-topic: ' . BUNDLE_ID,
      'authorization: bearer ' . generateAuthenticationHeader(),
      'apns-push-type: alert'
  ]);
}
```

Notice how you're explicitly telling `libcurl` that it should use the HTTP/2 protocol for this connection while passing your JWT as the authorization header. At this point, the session is open and signed, so you just need to loop through each token and send your payload across. Add the following code to the end of `sendNotifications()`:

```
$removeToken = $GLOBALS['db']->prepare('DELETE FROM apns WHERE
token = ?');
$server = $debug ? 'api.development' : 'api';
$tokens = tokensToReceiveNotification($debug);
```

This creates a PDO statement to remove a single token from the database, determines which APNs to connect to, and then queries all of the tokens using your previously defined function. You're almost done, keep going!

Add this final piece of PHP code inside `sendNotifications()`:

```
foreach ($tokens as $token) {
  // 1
  $url = "https://$server.push.apple.com/3/device/$token";
  curl_setopt($ch, CURLOPT_URL, "{$url}");

  // 2
  $response = curl_exec($ch);
  if ($response === false) {
    echo("curl_exec failed: " . curl_error($ch));
    continue;
  }
```

```
    // 3
    $code = curl_getinfo($ch, CURLINFO_HTTP_CODE);
    if ($code === 400 || $code === 410) {
      $json = @json_decode($response);
      if ($json->reason === 'BadDeviceToken') {
        $removeToken->execute([$token]);
      }
    }
  }

  curl_close($ch);
```

Here's what's happening in the preceding code:

1. You construct the actual URL to be used to send a notification to this token.
2. You try to submit the request to Apple over the cURL HTTP/2 Session you previously opened.
3. If Apple said something was wrong, and the reason was that the token was bad (`BadDeviceToken`), you remove this token from your database using the `$removeToken` PDO statement you prepared earlier. A token will become invalid if the user uninstalls your app.

Now all that you need to do is call the function! Add this code to the end of the file:

```
sendNotifications(true); // Development (Sandbox)
sendNotifications(false); // Production
?>
```

Depending on the way your development cycle works, you'll need to determine which type of tokens you're sending your push notifications to. At the start of development, when you're the only user, you'll just call `sendNotifications(true)`. Once you have some beta testers, you'll have to start calling it again with `false` so they get notifications. There will then be a period when both have to go out.

What happens when you finally push your app to the App Store? That's again dependent on your development flow.

While you continue to develop some other awesome features, you'll probably continue to send both Sandbox and Production notifications during your development and release cycle.

To run a PHP script, simply prepend the script name with `php` on the command line, like so:

```
$ php sendPushes.php
```

A PHP solution should support most server types.

If you don't have PHP installed on your machine, you can install it with Homebrew:

```
$ brew install php
```

What About JavaScript?

Another option would be using Node.js for your server, in which case you're not forced to add a PHP solution. There are multiple options on GitHub that you can use. For example, if you install the apn and pg modules using **Terminal**:

```
$ npm install apn --save
$ npm install pg --save
```

Your Node.js server could look a lot like this:

```
#!/usr/bin/env node

var apn = require('apn');
const { Client } = require('pg')

const options = {
  token: {
    key: '/full/path/to/AuthKey_keyid.p8',
    keyId: '',
    teamId: ''
  },
  production: false
}

const apnProvider = new apn.Provider(options);

var note = new apn.Notification();
note.expiry = Math.floor(Date.now() / 1000) + 3600; // 1 hour
note.badge = 3;
note.sound = "default";
note.alert = "Your alert here";
note.topic = "com.raywenderlich.PushNotifications";

const client = new Client({
  user: 'apns',
  host: 'localhost',
  database: 'apns',
  password: 'apns',
  port: 5433
})

client.connect()
```

```
client.query('SELECT DISTINCT token FROM tokens WHERE debug =
true', (err, res) => {
  client.end()

  const tokens = res.rows.map(row => row.token)

  apnProvider.send(note, tokens).then( (response) => {
    // response.sent has successful pushes
    // response.failed has error details
  });
})
```

But They Disabled Pushes!

You'll notice that you remove tokens from your database when a failure occurs. There's nothing there to handle the case where your user disables push notifications, nor should there be. Your user can toggle the status of push notifications at any time, and nothing requires them to go into the app to do that, since it's done from their device's Settings. Even if push notifications are disabled, it's still valid for Apple to send the push. The device simply ignores the push when it arrives.

> **Note**: Do *not* try detecting when pushes are off and removing the token. If the end-user goes into Settings and turns them back on, but doesn't run your app again for a while, they'll miss all the notifications they are expecting to receive!

Key Points

- You'll need to have a SQL server available to store device tokens.
- You'll need an API available to your iOS app to store and delete tokens.
- Do not use native Foundation network commands to send push notifications. Apple will consider that as a denial of service attack due to the repetitive opening and closing of connections.
- There are many options available for building your push server. Choose the one(s) that work best for your skillset.

Where to Go From Here?

As stated, if you are interested in learning more about the Vapor framework, you can check out our great set of videos (https://bit.ly/3n8bRLH) as well as our Vapor book, Server-Side Swift with Vapor (https://bit.ly/399PhxP).

There's also the Vapor documentation (https://docs.vapor.codes/) as well as a great community on Discord via the Vapor channel. To join the Discord group simply point your browser to vapor.team.

In the next chapter, "Expanding the Application," you'll configure your iOS app to talk to the server that you just configured.

Chapter 7: Expanding the Application

Now that you've got a database up and running, you need to tell your app how to connect to it. As you saw in the previous chapter, "Server Side Pushes," Vapor will run a local server for you at an address like **http://192.168.1.1:8080** (change with your own IP address).

This is the URL that your app will need to talk to if you successfully registered for push notifications. Of course, remember to substitute *your* IP address in the URL.

Token Details

You'll want to be able to pass appropriate details to your web service which describes the user's push notification registration.

Open the starter project from this chapter's materials, then create a new Swift file called **TokenDetails.swift** and add the following code:

```
struct TokenDetails {
  let token: String
  let debug: Bool
}
```

Your web service expects JSON data, so add an encoder to the top of the struct:

```
private let encoder = JSONEncoder()
```

To use the `JSONEncoder`, your `struct` must conform to `Encodable`. Add the following extension:

```
extension TokenDetails: Encodable {
  private enum CodingKeys: CodingKey {
    case token, debug
  }
}
```

You need to explicitly specify the `CodingKeys` because Swift, by default, will attempt to encode each property. You don't want to encode the encoder, though. By specifying the keys of *token* and *debug* Swift knows to only encode those two properties.

Now you can implement the method which will return the encoded data. Add the following inside `TokenDetails`:

```
func encoded() -> Data {
  return try! encoder.encode(self)
}
```

While fully functional, there's one more piece to implement. When you're debugging your app, you'll want to have an easy way to see what is being sent to the web service.

Add another extension:

```
extension TokenDetails: CustomStringConvertible {
  var description: String {
    return String(data: encoded(), encoding: .utf8) ?? "Invalid
token"
  }
}
```

`CustomStringConvertible` lets Swift know that when you pass this `struct` to `print` that it should call your custom implementation of the `description` property.

The last piece left is to add an initializer to `TokenDetails`:

```
init(token: Data) {
  self.token = token.reduce("") { $0 + String(format: "%02x",
$1) }

  #if DEBUG
    encoder.outputFormatting = .prettyPrinted
    debug = true
    print(String(describing: self))
  #else
    debug = false
  #endif
}
```

The `DEBUG` macro will be true when you're running your app from Xcode. Using the `.prettyPrinted` setting makes the JSON output more human friendly. As you add more items to the data that you send during registration, these "pretty" lines become a life saver when debugging.

You might, for example, want to store the users' preferred language. By storing the language on your server, you'll be able to periodically examine the list of languages to determine whether you should consider localizing your app to another language. Add a new property to `TokenDetails`:

```
let language: String
```

Then set the value in the initializer, just after assigning the token:

```
language = Locale.preferredLanguages[0]
```

Finally, add `language` to the `enum`:

```
case token, debug, language
```

Sending the Tokens

Now that you have a way to generate the details which will be sent, replace the `application(_:didRegisterForRemoteNotificationsWithDeviceToken:)` method body in **AppDelegate.swift** with the following code:

```
guard let url = URL(string: "http://192.168.1.1:8080/api/token")
else {
  fatalError("Invalid URL string")
}
```

You first declare the URL you'll send your token to. Remember to update the IP address with the IP of your Mac that you discovered in Chapter 6, "Server-Side Pushes".

Next, create an instance of `TokenDetails` in the method:

```
let details = TokenDetails(token: deviceToken)
```

Finally, finish the method by sending the request:

```
Task {
  var request = URLRequest(url: url)
  request.addValue("application/json", forHTTPHeaderField:
"Content-Type")
  request.httpMethod = "POST"
  request.httpBody = details.encoded()

  _ = try await URLSession.shared.data(for: request)
}
```

While `application(_:didRegisterForRemoteNotificationsWithDeviceToken:)` is not asynchronous, the `data(for:)` method is. By creating a new `Task` block you allow the delegate method to complete while the connection to your web server is handled in the background.

Notice that you're not checking the status of the request. If the registration with your web site or database were to fail for any reason, you wouldn't tell your end user this as there isn't anything they can do about it anyway. Hopefully, the next time they run your app, you would've fixed the server-side issue and the registration will complete successfully.

If you try to run this now, you'll get errors as Apple blocks the URL due to App Transport Security, or ATS. In a production app, you'd probably want to connect to secure website with the TLS protocol (i.e. *https* websites). Since this is only a development example, you can disable that security measurement.

Select **PushNotifications** at the top of the project window and then select the **PushNotifications** target. On the tab bar select **Info**. Add a new entry for **App Transport Security Settings** and then perform these three steps:

1. Expand your newly created **App Transport Security Settings** using the chevron on the left.
2. Right-click on **App Transport Security Settings** and choose **Add Row**.
3. Set the key to be **Allow Arbitrary Loads** and the value to be **YES**.

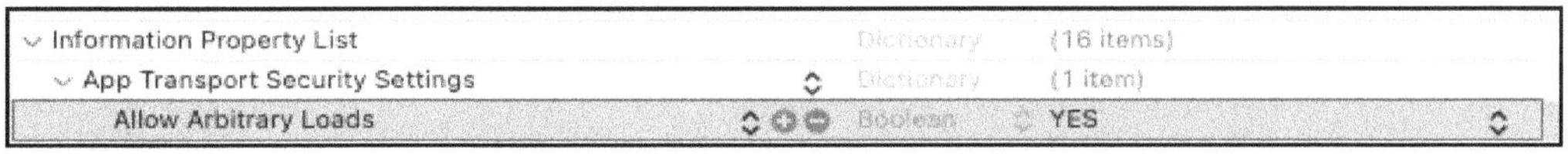

Testing

> **Note**: For this to work, you need to make sure an instance of your Vapor server is running and configured to run on your IP address, as well as make sure your database is running. You also need to set up the **sendPushes.php** script to use your APNs token. This is all described in Chapter 6, "Server-Side Pushes".

Build and run your app on a physical device. Put the app into the background by going to your home screen or locking your phone.

At this point, if you run the **sendPushes.php** script that you created in Chapter 6, "Server-Side Pushes," you should get a push notification!

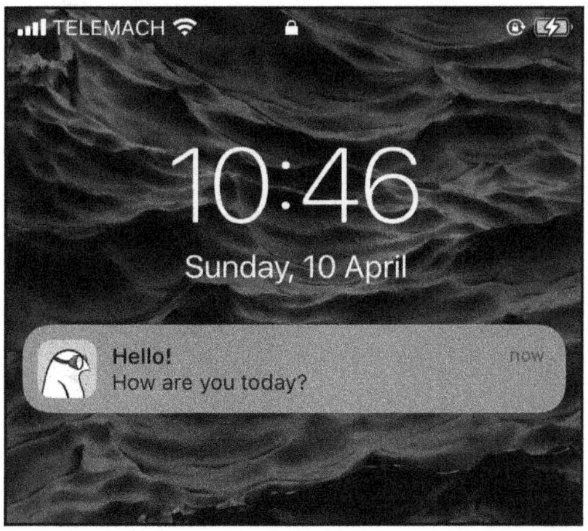

Refactor for Reuse

You can probably already see how the push notification code will be almost exactly the same in every project you create. Do a little cleanup by moving this common code to a new file called **PushNotifications**. Add the following code to the file:

```
import UIKit
import UserNotifications

enum PushNotifications {
  static func send(token: Data, to url: String) {
    guard let url = URL(string: url) else {
      fatalError("Invalid URL string")
    }

    Task {
      let details = TokenDetails(token: token)

      var request = URLRequest(url: url)
      request.addValue("application/json", forHTTPHeaderField:
"Content-Type")
      request.httpMethod = "POST"
      request.httpBody = details.encoded()

      _ = try await URLSession.shared.data(for: request)
    }
  }

  static func register(in application: UIApplication) {
    Task {
      let center = UNUserNotificationCenter.current()

      try await center.requestAuthorization(options:
[.badge, .sound, .alert])

      await MainActor.run {
        application.registerForRemoteNotifications()
      }
    }
  }
}
```

By using an `enum` you ensure that all of your methods are static and that you won't accidentally initialize an instance of `PushNotifications`.

Switch back to **AppDelegate.swift** and replace the class with the following simplified code:

```
class AppDelegate: NSObject, UIApplicationDelegate {
```

```
    func application(
      _ application: UIApplication,
      didFinishLaunchingWithOptions launchOptions:
      [UIApplication.LaunchOptionsKey: Any]?) -> Bool {

      PushNotifications.register(in: application)
      return true
    }

    func application(
      _ application: UIApplication,
      didRegisterForRemoteNotificationsWithDeviceToken
  deviceToken: Data) {

      PushNotifications.send(token: deviceToken, to: "http://
  192.168.1.1:8080")
    }
  }
```

You could, of course, leave the code in **AppDelegate.swift**. However, many of your apps will have other requirements for the application delegate unrelated to push notifications. By extracting that code into a file of its own you make future projects easier to configure. Simply copy the **PushNotifications.swift** file into the project and add a line to the appropriate delegate methods.

Key Points

- Once you have your database established, you need to tell your app how to connect to it. Vapor will allow you to run a server written with Swift.
- Take the time to add some additional lines at the end of notification registration to display the body of the JSON request in a "pretty," easy-to-read format, which can help in the future with debugging.

Where to Go From Here?

And there you have it! You've successfully built an API that saves device tokens and an app that consumes that API. This is the basic skeleton you will build upon when using push notifications. In Chapter 8, "Handling Common Scenarios," you will start handling common push notification scenarios, such as displaying a notification while the app is in the foreground... so keep reading!

Chapter 8: Handling Common Scenarios

So far you learned how to receive remote push notifications from APNs. iOS then takes over and shows the notification to the user. However, that's not the full story. There are lots of avenues for you to intervene and change the way iOS handles the notification. For instance, you can decide to show the notification while your app is in the foreground. You can also decide what happens when your user taps the notification. Or, you can hide the notification from your user entirely. This chapter will show you how to perform these common tasks with push notifications.

Displaying Foreground Notifications

As you noticed in previous projects in this book, iOS will automatically handle presenting your notifications as long as your app is in the background or terminated. But what happens when it is actively running? In that case, you need to decide what it is that you want to happen. By default, iOS simply eats the notification and never displays it. That's pretty much always what you want to happen, right? No? Didn't think so!

In the download materials for this chapter, you'll find possibly the coolest starter project that's ever been created.

```
sarcasm
'sär-ˌka-zəm
noun
the use of irony to mock or convey contempt
```

If you'd like to have iOS display your notification while your app is running in the foreground, you'll need to implement the `UNUserNotificationCenterDelegate` method `userNotificationCenter(_:willPresent:withCompletionHandler:)`, which is called when a notification is delivered to your app while it's in the foreground. The only requirement of this method is calling the completion handler before it returns. Here, you can identify what you want to happen when the notification comes in.

Open the starter project from this chapter's download materials. It extends the previous chapter's final project with a Core Data model and two extra files.

You are able to configure parts of the notification via a `UNUserNotificationCenterDelegate`. To support a delegate, replace the `register(in:)` method back in **PushNotifications.swift** with this method:

```
static func register(
  in application: UIApplication,
  // 1
  using notificationDelegate: UNUserNotificationCenterDelegate?
= nil
) {
  Task {
    let center = UNUserNotificationCenter.current()

    try await center.requestAuthorization(options:
[.badge, .sound, .alert])

    // 2
    center.delegate = notificationDelegate
```

```
      await MainActor.run {
        application.registerForRemoteNotifications()
      }
    }
  }
```

You made two simple changes:

1. The method now accepts an optional delegate.
2. You assigned the `UNUserNotificationCenter`'s delegate to be the supplied delegate.

The delegate you will implement is pretty simple. Create a new file, **NotificationCenter.swift** and replace the file's contents with the following code:

```
import UserNotifications

final class NotificationCenter: NSObject {
}

extension NotificationCenter: UNUserNotificationCenterDelegate {
  func userNotificationCenter(
    _ center: UNUserNotificationCenter,
    willPresent notification: UNNotification
  ) async -> UNNotificationPresentationOptions {
    return [.banner, .sound, .badge]
  }
}
```

Probably one of the most complex methods you've ever written, right? In just a bit you'll need this class to conform to `NSObject` so I'm simply having you define it that way now.

The method you implemented gets called by iOS when it is about to show a notification. In the method, you're telling the app that you want the normal alert to be displayed, the sound played and the badge updated. If the notification doesn't have one of these components, or the user has disabled any of them, that part is simply ignored.

It used to be that you'd specify `.alert` if you wanted the notification to display to the end user. As of iOS 14, Apple provides you the ability to decide whether or not you'd like the alert to display when the app is in the foreground. If you do want foreground notifications, choose the `.banner` enum value. If you only wish alerts to appear when the app is running in the background, use `.list`.

If you want no action to happen, you can simply pass an empty array to the completion closure. Depending on the logic that pertains to your app, you may want to investigate the `notification.request` property of type `UNNotificationRequest` and make the decision about which components to show based on the notification that was sent to you.

Finally, back in **AppDelegate.swift**, add a new property to the class:

```
let notificationCenter = NotificationCenter()
```

And then update the `register(in:)` call to utilize the delegate:

```
PushNotifications.register(in: application, using:
notificationCenter)
```

Build and run your app. Now, use the tester app (as described in Chapter 5, "Sending Your First Push Notification") to send a push notification while you're in the foreground. You should see it displayed this time! You can use the following simple payload for testing purposes:

```
{
  "aps": {
    "alert": {
      "title": "Hello Foreground!",
      "body": "This notification appeared in the foreground."
    }
  }
}
```

You should get a notification on your device with your app still in the foreground!

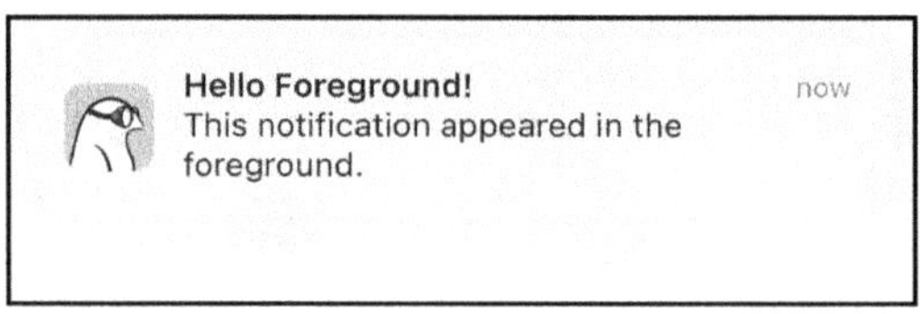

Tapping the Notification

The vast majority of the time when a push notification arrives, your end users won't do anything except glance at it. Good notifications don't **require** interaction, and your user gets what they need at a glance. However, that's not always the case. Sometimes your users actually tap on the notification, which will trigger your app to be launched.

Handling User Interaction

By default, tapping on the notification simply opens up your app to whatever the “current” screen was — or the default startup screen, if the app was launched from a terminated state.

Sometimes, that’s not what you want though, as the notification should take you to a specific view within your app. Add the following property to the `NotificationCenter` class:

```
@Published var isBeachViewActive = false
```

Then, tell the class to conform to the `ObservableObject` protocol:

```
extension NotificationCenter: ObservableObject {}
```

Now, inside the extension, add the delegate method to handle taps:

```
func userNotificationCenter(
  _ center: UNUserNotificationCenter,
  didReceive response: UNNotificationResponse
) async {
  if response.notification.request.content.userInfo["beach"] !=
nil {
    // In a real app you'd likely pull a URL from the beach data
    // and use that image.
    await MainActor.run {
      isBeachViewActive = true
    }
  }
}
```

The keys sent with the push notification are inside the `userInfo` property, a simple Swift dictionary. If you find a value with the key `"beach"`, set the published property to `true`. You can see how, in a more dynamic setup, the `userInfo` might contain a URL to an image that you may then need to download. You’ll handle a case similar to this later in this book.

Remember that `userNotificationCenter(_:didReceive:)` is not called on the main thread, and so you must delegate back to the main thread via the `await MainActor.run` call.

Hop over to **PushNotificationsApp.swift**. Add the following line at the end of `body`, right under the `environment` call:

```
.environmentObject(appDelegate.notificationCenter)
```

This will give all child views access to the notification delegate, including `ContentView`, which you'll update next.

Jump over to **ContentView.swift** and add a new property to the struct:

```
@EnvironmentObject var notificationCenter: NotificationCenter
```

This will grab the notification delegate you just added to the app struct.

Finally, add the following code to `body`, at the bottom of `NavigationStack`:

```
if notificationCenter.isBeachViewActive {
  BeachView()
}
```

When the newly created property in `NotificationCenter` gets set to `true`, you will show the beach view.

Build and run your app, then send yourself a test push with the following payload:

```
{
  "beach": true,
  "aps": {
    "alert": {
      "body": "Tap me!"
    }
  }
}
```

Once the notification is presented, tap it. If all goes well, you should be presented with the `BeachView` instantiated above:

Sending Silent Notifications

Sometimes, when you send a notification, you don't want the user to actually get a visual cue when it comes in. No alert or sound, for example.

These are generally referred to as **silent notifications**, but what they really mean is, "Hey app, there's new content available on the server you might need to do something with."

If you've written an RSS reader app, for example, you might send a silent notification when a new post is submitted so that the app can prefetch the data.

This makes the user's app experience much quicker as the data is there as soon as the app is opened, versus the end user watching an activity indicator while the article is being downloaded.

There are three distinct steps you have to take in order to enable silent notifications:

1. Update the payload.
2. Add the **Background Modes** capability.
3. Implement a new `UIApplicationDelegate` method.

Updating the Payload

The first step to take is simply adding a new key-value pair to your payload. Inside of the `aps` dictionary, add a new key of `content-available` with a value of `1`. This will tell iOS to wake your app when it receives a push notification, so it can prefetch any content related to the notification.

In this case, you're going to have your app prefetch an image. To start, create a payload like so:

```
{
  "aps": {
    "content-available": 1
  },
  "image": "https://bit.ly/3dfsW2n",
  "text": "A nice picture of the Earth"
}
```

You can use any image URL you'd like. The above is just a known image that should always resolve.

> **Note**: Don't set the value to `0` thinking you've disabled this. If you don't want a silent notification — do not include the `content-available` key!

> **Note**: Remember to set the `apns-priority` HTTP header to 5, as explained in Chapter 3.

Adding Background Modes Capability

Next, back in Xcode, you'll need to add a new capability just as you did at project creation.

Open the project navigator (⌘ + 1), select your project and then select your app target.

Now, on the **Signing & Capabilities** tab, press the **+ Capability** button and add the **Background Modes** capability. From the **Background Modes** options check the **Remote notifications** checkbox.

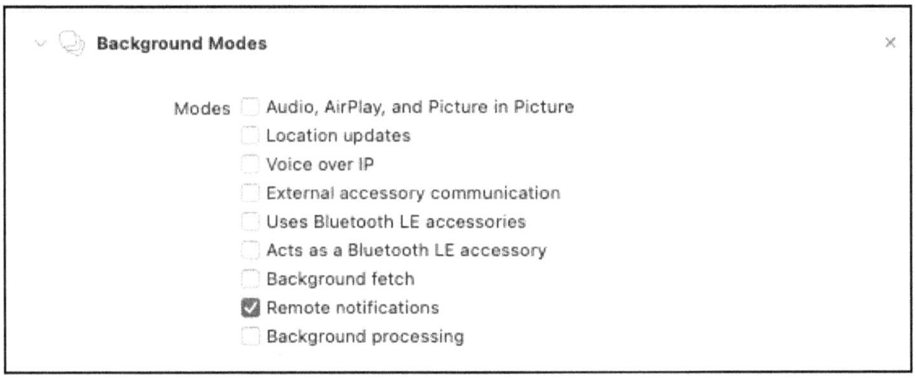

App Delegate Updates

When a silent notification comes in, you'll want to make sure that it contains the data you're expecting, updates your Core Data model, and then tells iOS you're done processing.

You'll need to implement a new `AppDelegate` method by adding following code in **AppDelegate.swift**:

```
func application(
```

```
    _ application: UIApplication,
    didReceiveRemoteNotification userInfo: [AnyHashable : Any])
    async -> UIBackgroundFetchResult {
  guard
    let text = userInfo["text"] as? String,
    let image = userInfo["image"] as? String,
    let url = URL(string: image)
  else {
    completionHandler(.noData)
    return
  }
}
```

This method gets called whenever a push notification comes in, including when your app is in the background. You are expecting both `text` and an `image` as part of the payload, and you need to ensure that the image specified is actually something you can turn into a `URL`.

If there is any issues, you can tell iOS that you don't have the needed data by returning `.noData`. You probably don't want to specify `.failed` since technically this just wasn't a payload for an image.

Since you're about to update Core Data objects you'll need to import the appropriate module at the top of the file:

```
import CoreData
```

Next, add the following code below the `guard` statement in the method:

```
let context = PersistenceController.shared.container.viewContext

do {
  // 1
  let (imageData, _) = try await URLSession.shared.data(from:
url)
  // 2
  return try await context.perform(schedule: .immediate) { ()
throws -> UIBackgroundFetchResult in
    // 3
    let message = Message(context: context)
    message.image = imageData
    message.received = Date()
    message.text = text

    try context.save()
    // 4
    return .newData
  }
} catch {
```

```
    // 5
    return .failed
}
```

Here's what's going on in the code:

1. First, fetch the image data from the URL.
2. Which thread is your notification running on? Not sure? Play it safe and make sure the Core Data operations run on the proper thread of your Core Data persistent container.
3. Create a new `Message` object wit the downloaded image.
4. Since you did, in fact, receive data, tell iOS that you got new data from this notification, and that you were able to successfully process the notification.
5. If anything went wrong, tell iOS that processing the notification failed.

> **Note**: iOS will wake up your app in the background and give it up to 30 seconds to complete whatever actions you need to take. Make sure you perform the minimal amount of work necessary so that your action can complete in time.

Build and run the project.

Send yourself a few more silent push notifications using different images and text, and you should see your table updating appropriately.

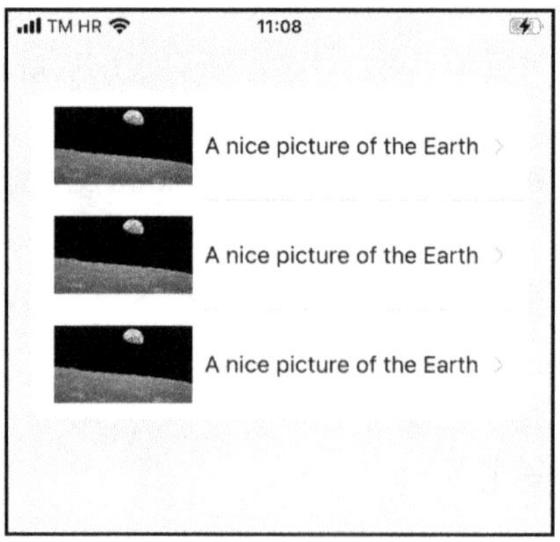

Method Routing

The following table shows you which methods are called, and in what order, depending on whether your app is in the foreground or background, and whether or not the `content-available` flag (i.e., silent notification) is present with a value of `1`.

Foreground	content-available	Storage size
Yes	No	userNotificationCenter(:willPresent:)
Yes	Yes	userNotificationCenter(:willPresent:) application(:didReceiveRemoteNotification:)
No	No	userNotificationCenter(:willPresent:)
No	Yes	application(:didReceiveRemoteNotification:)

Key Points

- For iOS to display your notification while your app is running in the foreground, you'll need to implement a `UNUserNotificationCenterDelegate` method, which is called when a notification is delivered to your app while it's in the foreground.
- Good notifications don't require interaction, and your user gets what they need at a glance. Some notifications are tapped, however, which triggers an app launch. You will need to add an additional method in your **AppDelegate.swift** file.
- Sometimes, you want a tapped notification to open a specific view controller within your app. You will need to add an additional method to handle this routing.
- **Silent notifications** give no visual or audible cue. To enable silent notifications, you'll need to update the payload, add the Background Modes capability, and implement a new `UIApplicationDelegate method`.

Chapter 9: Custom Actions

At this point, you've implemented as much of push notifications as most app developers will ever want or need to do. Don't give up now! There are still some really amazing features you can add to your app to make it shine, should you so desire.

In the previous chapter, you built an app that triggers an action when the user taps on a received notification. Sometimes, a simple tap is not enough. Maybe your friend is asking you to grab coffee and you want an easy way to accept the offer. Or maybe another friend posted a funny tweet and you want to favorite it right from the notification.

Thankfully, iOS gives you a way to attach buttons to a push notification so that the user can provide a meaningful response to the received notification without having to open your app! In this chapter, you'll learn how to make your notifications actionable.

Adding Categories

Notification categories allow you to specify up to four custom actions per category that will be displayed with your push notification. Keep in mind that the system will only display the first two actions if your notification appears in a banner, so you always want to configure the most relevant actions first.

> **Note**: The simulator does not currently display categories. Be sure to test on a physical device.

To enable the user to decide what action to take, you'll add **Accept** and **Reject** buttons to your push notifications.

Open the starter project from this chapter's materials. In **PushNotifications.swift**, at the top of the `enum` add a couple lines to identify your buttons:

```
public static let categoryIdentifier = "AcceptOrReject"

public enum ActionIdentifier: String {
  case accept, reject
}
```

Use an `enum` to ensure you aren't hardcoding strings for identifiers as you won't ever display them to an end user. Once that's done, add a method at the bottom of `PushNotifications` to perform the registration.

```
static func registerCustomActions() {
  let accept = UNNotificationAction(
    identifier: ActionIdentifier.accept.rawValue,
    title: "Accept")

  let reject = UNNotificationAction(
    identifier: ActionIdentifier.reject.rawValue,
    title: "Reject")

  let category = UNNotificationCategory(
    identifier: Self.categoryIdentifier,
    actions: [accept, reject],
    intentIdentifiers: [])


UNUserNotificationCenter.current().setNotificationCategories([ca
tegory])
}
```

Here, you create a notification category with two buttons. When a push notification arrives with a category set to `AcceptOrReject`, your custom actions will be triggered, and iOS will include the two buttons at the bottom of your push notification.

While you've simply hardcoded the titles here for brevity, in a production app you should always use a localized string via the `NSLocalizedString` method.

> **Note**: Even if you don't think you're going to localize your app, it's better to get in the habit now than have to go back and find every single user visible string later if plans change!

You only need to register your actions if you're actually accepting push notifications, so add a call to `registerCustomActions()` at the end of `application(_:didRegisterForRemoteNotificationsWithDeviceToken:)` in **AppDelegate.swift**:

```
PushNotifications.registerCustomActions()
```

Build and run your app. Now, go back into the push notification tester app (as described in Chapter 5, "Sending Your First Push Notification") and use the following payload:


```
{
  "aps": {
    "alert": {
      "title": "Long-press this notification"
    },
    "category": "AcceptOrReject",
    "sound": "default"
  }
}
```


The critical part of the payload is making sure the `category` value **exactly** matches what you specified during your registration with `UNUserNotificationCenter`. Send another push to yourself now.

See your action buttons? No? Don't worry, you didn't mess anything up!

The trick is you need to long press the notification to reveal the buttons.

Once you do that, the custom buttons appear and you can select one.

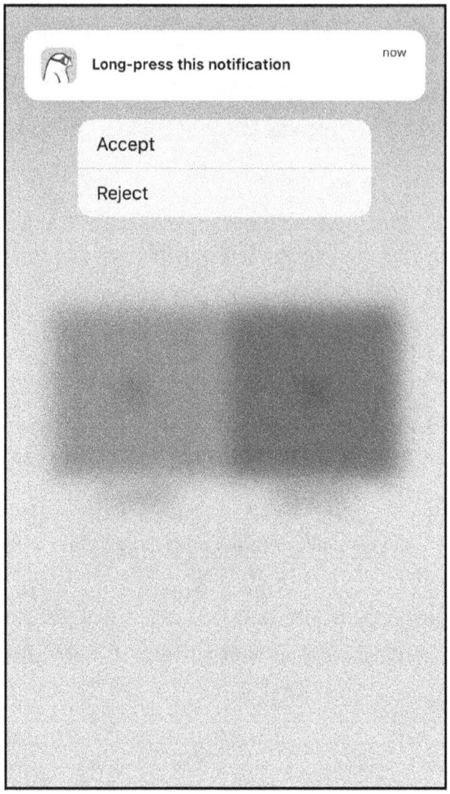

However, currently pressing the buttons doesn't do anything. You'll fix that next.

Go back into your **NotificationCenter.swift** and add the following method inside the extension:

```
@MainActor
internal func userNotificationCenter(
  _ center: UNUserNotificationCenter,
  didReceive response: UNNotificationResponse
) async {
  let identity =
response.notification.request.content.categoryIdentifier
  guard identity == PushNotifications.categoryIdentifier,
    let action = PushNotifications.ActionIdentifier(rawValue:
response.actionIdentifier) else {
    return
  }

  print("You pressed \(response.actionIdentifier)")
}
```

> **Note**: You can safely ignore the warning about `action` not being used as you'll use it in just a moment.

Remember that this method will be called when you tap on the notification, so you need to do a quick check to make sure you're handling your own category, and then you can grab the button that was pressed. This method will be called even when your app is not in the foreground, so be careful of what you do here!

This is an async method that needs to be called from the main thread, so you add the `@MainActor` property wrapper so that you can safely trigger UI updates from the method.

Build and run your code again, and send yourself another notification from the Tester app. Long press the notification and select one of the buttons; you should see the following message in Xcode's console:

```
You pressed accept
```

Tracking the Notification With Combine

The `NotificationCenter` is not where you want to take action when a push notification is acted upon, unless it's a simple data storage operation. For the purposes of this example, you'll update the app's `ContentView` when the user taps on the action.

Create a new Swift file named **Counter.swift** and paste this code into it:

```
import Combine

// 1
final class Counter: ObservableObject {
  // 2
  @Published public var accepted = 0
  @Published public var rejected = 0

  // 3
  static let shared = Counter()

  private init() {}
}
```

Combine may be a new framework for you if you're just getting started with SwiftUI programming. The above class has three simple parts:

1. Previously you may have used Foundation's Notification Center to signal changes to other parts of your code. A better option is subclassing `ObservableObject`.
2. You've annotated two variables with the `@Published` property wrapper so that other sections of your code can *observe* when `accepted` or `rejected` change values.
3. You'll use this class as a singleton.

SwiftUI allows you to use the `@EnvironmentObject` property wrapper to place an `ObservableObject` into the environment. However, you're going to need to use the `Counter` class in plain old `NSObject` classes, which don't support `@EnvironmentObject`. By making the class a singleton it'll be available everywhere you need it.

Responding to the Action

Head back over to the **NotificationCenter.swift** file and replace the `print` statement with the following code:

```
switch action {
case .accept: Counter.shared.accepted += 1
case .reject: Counter.shared.rejected += 1
}
```

Now that you've properly detected that your end user has selected a custom action, and you've posted the notification, you need to actually *do* something. Return to **ContentView.swift**. You'll see that the counters are currently based on local state. Delete both `@State` variables, replacing it with this line:

```
@ObservedObject var counter = Counter.shared
```

By using the `@ObservedObject` property wrapper you've let SwiftUI know that it needs to watch for any published changes to the object.

Finally, replace the bindings on the `ColoredCounter` lines to point to the object you're observing:

```
ColoredCounter(
  count: $counter.accepted,
  backgroundColor: .green,
  text: "Accepted")

ColoredCounter(
  count: $counter.rejected,
  backgroundColor: .red,
  text: "Rejected")
```

Build and run the app one final time. Send yourself a bunch of notifications, alternating between which button you tap each time. The display should keep a count for you!

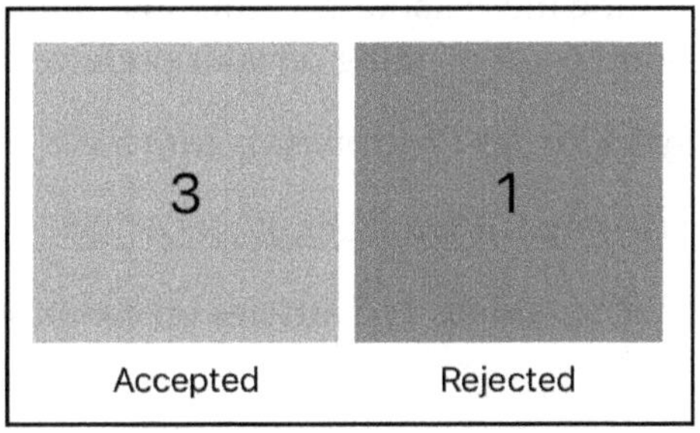

By using the Combine framework, you've kept the logic of your app encapsulated into the right areas, and you haven't gone through convolutions to let the `UNUserNotificationCenterDelegate` methods know anything about the view controllers, which might or might not want to take action based on a notification.

Making notifications actionable is a good idea whenever it makes sense, as it streamlines the experience for the user and makes their life a little bit easier. Another added benefit is the fact these actions are also automatically displayed for users of the Apple Watch!

Key Points

- You can make a push notification actionable by attaching a button to a notification.
- Notification categories allow you to specify up to four custom actions per category that will be displayed with your push notification.
- Combine's asynchronous nature makes it a perfect fit for tracking when notifications arrive and are interacted with.

Where to Go From Here?

If you're interested in learning more about the Combine framework, you can check out any of these great resources, depending on your preferred learning style:

- Our book, *Combine: Asynchronous Programming with Swift*, at bit.ly/3k3n8LT.
- Our tutorial, *Combine: Getting Started*, at bit.ly/2FGWHwG.
- Any of our hundreds of other videos and articles on combine at bit.ly/3o2Fxeg.

Chapter 10: Modifying the Payload

Sometimes, you'll need to take extra steps before a notification is presented to the user. For example, you may wish to download an image or change the text of a notification.

In the **DidIWin** lottery app, for example, you'd want the notification to tell the user exactly how much money they have won. Given the push notification simply contains today's drawing numbers, you'll be using a **Notification Service Extension** to intercept those numbers and apply logic to them.

You can think of a Notification Service Extension as middleware between APNs and your UI. With it, you can receive a remote notification and modify its content before it's presented to the user. Considering the fact notification payloads are limited in size, this can be a very useful trick! Another common use case for modifying the payload is if you're sending encrypted data to your app. The service extension is where you'd decrypt the data so that it's properly displayed to your end user.

In this chapter, you'll go over what it takes to build a Notification Service app extension and how to implement some of its most common use cases.

Configuring Xcode for a Service Extension

Due to your proven track record of writing amazing apps, your country's spy agency has contracted you to write the app that its field agents will use to receive updates from headquarters. Of course, the agency sends all of its data using massive encryption, so you'll need to handle the decryption for the agents. Nobody wants to read a gobbledygook text!

Open the starter project for this chapter. Remember to set the team signing as discussed in Chapter 7, "Expanding the Application."

Gibberish

Build and run your app, and send yourself a push notification with the following payload:

```
{
  "aps": {
    "alert": {
      "title": "Lbhe Gnetrg",
      "body": "Guvf vf lbhe arkg nffvtazrag."
    },
    "sound": "default",
    "badge": 1,
    "mutable-content": 1
  },
  "media-url":
          "uggcf://jbyirevar.enljraqreyvpu.pbz/obbxf/abg/
ohaal.zc4"
}
```

If everything goes correctly, you should see a notification on your device. However, this notification is encrypted by the agency, and you need to decrypt the contents before displaying the notification on the device.

Creating the Service Extension

You need to add a service extension target so that you can handle the encryption being used.

1. In Xcode, select **File ▸ New ▸ Target...**.
2. Make sure **iOS** is selected and choose the **Notification Service Extension**.
3. For the product name specify **Payload Modification**.
4. Press **Finish**.
5. When asked about scheme activation, select **Cancel**.

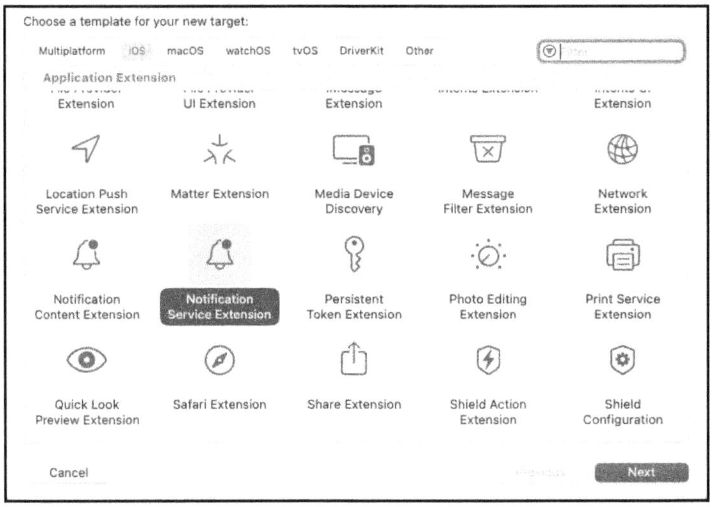

> **Note**: You don't actually *run* a service extension so that's why you didn't let it make the new target your active scheme.

You can name the new target anything that makes sense for you, but it can be helpful to use the above name because, when you glance at your project, you will immediately know what that target is doing.

If you look in the Project navigator (⌘ + 1), you'll see you now have a new folder group called **Payload Modification**. You'll notice that there's a **NotificationService.swift** file but no views. This is because service extensions don't present any type of UI. They are called *before* the UI is presented, be it yours or the one Apple displays for you. You'll get into UI modifications in the next chapter.

Decrypting the Payload

As mentioned at the start of the chapter, the payload you receive has encrypted the data. Your country is a little bit behind the times though, and it is still using the **ROT13** letter substitution cipher in which each letter is simply replaced by the letter 13 places further along in the alphabet, wrapping back to the beginning of the alphabet if necessary.

In your **Payload Modification** target create a new Swift file named **ROT13.swift** and paste this code into it:

```
import Foundation

struct ROT13 {
  static let shared = ROT13()

  private let upper = Array("ABCDEFGHIJKLMNOPQRSTUVWXYZ")
  private let lower = Array("abcdefghijklmnopqrstuvwxyz")
  private var mapped: [Character: Character] = [:]

  private init() {
    for i in 0 ..< 26 {
      let idx = (i + 13) % 26
      mapped[upper[i]] = upper[idx]
      mapped[lower[i]] = lower[idx]
    }
  }

  public func decrypt(_ str: String) -> String {
    return String(str.map { mapped[$0] ?? $0 })
  }
}
```

You can find many different ways of implementing this cipher in Swift. The above is just a quick and dirty way to handle the American English alphabet.

Obviously, the above code makes a nice sample for a book as it doesn't require downloads and configuration. However, for real security, you should look to something like the CryptoSwift (cryptoswift.io) library.

Open the **NotificationService.swift** file and you'll see a bit of content already provided for you by Apple. The first method in this file, `didReceive(_:withContentHandler:)` is called when your notification arrives. You have *roughly* 30 seconds to perform whatever actions you need to take. If you run out of time, iOS will call the second method, `serviceExtensionTimeWillExpire` to give you one last chance to hurry up and finish.

If you're using a restartable network connection, the second method might give you just enough time to finish. Don't try to perform the same actions again in the `serviceExtensionTimeWillExpire` method though. The intent of this method is that you perform a much smaller change that can happen quickly. You may have a slow network connection, for example, so there's no point in trying yet another network download. Instead, it might be a good idea to tell the user that they got a new image or a new video, even if you didn't get a chance to download it.

> **Note**: If you haven't called the completion handler before time runs out, iOS will continue on with the original payload.

You may make any modification to the payload you want — except for one. You may not remove the alert text. If you don't have alert text, then iOS will ignore your modifications and proceed with the original payload.

Now, back in your **NotificationService.swift** file, find the lines in `didReceive(_:withContentHandler:)` that show an example modification:

```
// Modify the notification content here...
bestAttemptContent.title = "\(bestAttemptContent.title)
[modified]"
```

Replace them with code to decrypt the data:

```
bestAttemptContent.title =
ROT13.shared.decrypt(bestAttemptContent.title)
bestAttemptContent.body =
ROT13.shared.decrypt(bestAttemptContent.body)
```

Build and run your app again on a physical device, then send yourself the same push notification again.

> **Note**: Simulator will not currently run a service extension.

If everything worked correctly, you should see a decrypted push notification appear on your phone.

What happened here is that iOS has noticed that your app has a Notification Service Extension, and it has called the method you just modified before it displayed the notification. In the method, you changed the notification's content, and iOS has then displayed the modified notification to the user. This all happened without ever launching your main app target.

Downloading a Video

Service extensions are also the place in which you can download videos or other content from the internet. First, you need to find the URL of the attached media. Once you have that, you can try to download it into a temporary directory somewhere on the user's device. Once you have the data, you can create a `UNNotificationAttachment` object, which you can attach to the actual notification.

Go back to **NotificationService.swift** and replace the whole `if` statement and block the following code:

```
guard let bestAttemptContent else {
  return
}

bestAttemptContent.title =
ROT13.shared.decrypt(bestAttemptContent.title)
bestAttemptContent.body =
ROT13.shared.decrypt(bestAttemptContent.body)
```

Using a `guard` statement is usually preferable to wrapping an entire method in a conditional check. After your statements that replace the title and body of the push notification, you'll now need to check and see if there's media to download. Add these lines of code:

```
guard
  let urlPath = request.content.userInfo["media-url"] as?
String,
  let url = URL(string: ROT13.shared.decrypt(urlPath))
else {
  contentHandler(bestAttemptContent)
  return
}
```

You're first checking to determine whether the payload includes the **media-url** key. If it does, you then decrypt the URL just as you did for the title and body. Finally, you then attempt to convert that to an actual `URL` object. If any of the checks failed then there are no other actions which need to be performed so you call the completion handler and exit the method.

> **Note**: You didn't call the completion handler inside the first `guard` statement as you didn't have content at that point. In the second `guard` you've already updated the title and body, so now you must call the completion handler.

Now it's time to download the media, using the following code:

```
Task {
  // 1
  defer { contentHandler(bestAttemptContent) }

  do {
    // 2
    let (data, response) = try await
```

```
URLSession.shared.data(from: url)
    // 3
    let file = response.suggestedFilename ??
url.lastPathComponent
    let destination = URL(fileURLWithPath:
NSTemporaryDirectory())
      .appendingPathComponent(file)
    try data.write(to: destination)
    // 4
    let attachment = try UNNotificationAttachment(
          identifier: "",
          url: destination)
    bestAttemptContent.attachments = [attachment]
    contentHandler(bestAttemptContent)
  } catch {
    // 5
    print("An error occurred.")
  }
}
```

Here's what the above code is doing:

1. It's critical to call the content handler, so a `defer` statement is a great choice here.
2. Download the media using `data(from:)` instead of `download(from:)`. The latter method will handle creating the file on your device but the filename extension will not be correct.
3. You'll need to write the downloaded data to a file, but not just any temporary file. The extension for the file must be correct for iOS to know how to display the media. If the provider specified a filename, use that. Otherwise, just take the end of the URL path.
4. Once you've written the data to disk, you create a `UNNotificationAttachment`. iOS will generate a unique identifier for you if you leave it empty. Finally, add the attachment to the content of the push notification.
5. There's not really anything you can do if the download fails, so you'll just print out an error message.

Notice how the method ends at that point, yet you didn't call the completion handler. The data download is an asynchronous action, meaning the method will end before the download completes. That's OK because you ensured, via the `defer` statement, that the completion handler will be called when the download exits.

Build and run your app again, and then resend the same push notification.

You should get a push notification that has a small image on the right-hand side. Long-press the notification and you'll see a video with your next target!

Service Extension Payloads

You don't necessarily always want an extension to run every time you receive a push notification — just when it needs to be modified. In the above example, you'd obviously use it 100% of the time as you're decrypting data. But what if you were just downloading a video? You don't **always** send videos.

To tell iOS that the service extension should be used, simply add a `mutable-content` key to the `aps` dictionary with an integer value of `1`.

> **Note**: If you forget to add this key, your service extension will never be called. You're most likely going to forget to do this and have a heck of a time figuring out why your code doesn't work!

Sharing Data With Your Main Target

Your primary app target and your extension are two separate processes. You can't share data between them by default. If you do more than the most simplistic of things with your extension, you'll quickly find yourself wanting to be able to pass data back and forth. This is easily accomplished via **Application Groups**, which allows access to group containers that are shared between multiple related apps and extensions.

To enable this capability, press ⌘ + 1 to go back to the **Project navigator** and click on your main target. Next, navigate to the **Signing & Capabilities** tab again. Click the **+ Capability** button in the top-left and you'll see **App Groups** near the top of the list. Double-click it.

You should see a new section pop up called **App Groups** in the tab. Press the **+** button and then set the name you wish to use. Generally, you'll want the same name as your bundle identifier, just prefixed with `group`:

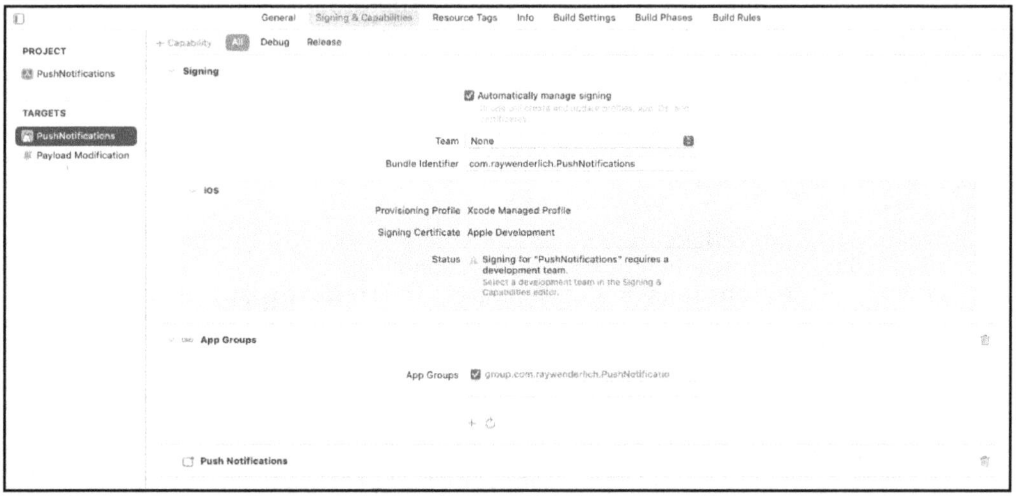

Now, go into your **Payload Modification** target's capabilities tab and enable the App Groups there as well, selecting the same app group you selected for your app target.

Badging the App Icon

A great use for service extensions is to handle the app badge. As discussed in Chapter 3, "Remote Notification Payload", iOS will set the badge to *exactly* what you specify in the payload, if you provide a number. What happens if the end user has ignored your notifications so far? Maybe you've sent them three new items at this point. You'd rather the badge said `3` and not `1`, right?

Historically, app developers have sent information back to the server as to how many badges the app icon is currently displaying, and then the push notification would increment that number by one. While that's doable, it's quite a bit of extra overhead to deal with on your server. By utilizing a service extension, you can now just pretend that the badge key being there means to increment the badge count by that number. You're now just storing locally how many items are unread versus having to send those details back to your server for tracking.

As this is just an integer value, you can make use of the `UserDefaults` class with one small change — assuming you've already enabled App Groups. You have to specify the suite that is used to enable it to span targets. To do so, add a new Swift file to your **primary target**, not the extension, called **UserDefaults.swift**:

```
import Foundation

extension UserDefaults {
  // 1
  static let suiteName =
"group.com.yourcompany.PushNotifications"
  static let extensions = UserDefaults(suiteName: suiteName)!
  // 2
  private enum Keys {
    static let badge = "badge"
  }
  // 3
  var badge: Int {
    get { UserDefaults.extensions.integer(forKey: Keys.badge) }
    set { UserDefaults.extensions.set(newValue, forKey:
Keys.badge) }
  }
}
```

1. First, you define a new `extensions` property, providing a `UserDefaults` object you'd use when you want to share your defaults between targets. Change the `suitName` to be the ID of the App Group you selected in your targets.
2. Hardcoding strings is a bad idea, so you create an `enum` with a static `let` so that you only have to do it once. A `struct` would work here just as well. The reason you want to use an `enum` is that you can't accidentally instantiate it.
3. Finally, you wrap up by creating a computed property for `badge` that handles the get/set. Again, this is just good coding style to make life easier on the caller.

Right now, this file is only accessible from the main target though. Bring up the **File inspector** by pressing ⌥ + ⌘ + 1 and in the **Target Membership** section check the boxes next to your service extension as well as the primary target:

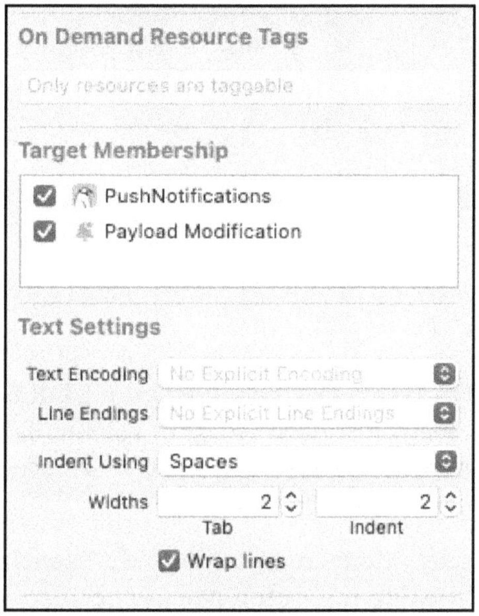

Now, back in **NotificationService.swift**, edit the `didReceive(_:withContentHandler:)` method. You can check for badging information by placing the following code just before you assign the title and body:

```
if let increment = bestAttemptContent.badge as? Int {
  if increment == 0 {
    UserDefaults.extensions.badge = 0
    bestAttemptContent.badge = 0
  } else {
    let current = UserDefaults.extensions.badge
    let new = current + increment
```

```
        UserDefaults.extensions.badge = new
        bestAttemptContent.badge = NSNumber(value: new)
    }
}
```

It's important to store the value to a `UserDefaults` type structure so you modify that value in your primary target as well. When your user accesses the part of your app that the badge refers to, you'll want to decrement the badge count so that the app icon is updated.

Build and run the app. Send yourself push notifications a few times and the badge number should increase for each notification you receive:

Accessing Core Data

Writing to a `UserDefaults` key can be incredibly useful, but isn't normally good enough. Sometimes, you really just need access to your actual app's data store in your extension. Most commonly, you'll look for a way to access Core Data. It's easy enough to do once you've enabled App Groups.

First, select your data model (**Model.xcdatamodeld**). Then, in the **Target Membership** section of the **File inspector**, add a checkmark next to your service notification target. If you created any `NSManagedObject` subclasses that you need to use, do the same thing with them.

Second, edit your **Persistence.swift** file, making a small change to the container setup. You've got to tell the container exactly where to store the data. Replace the `if inMemory` check with this:

```
let url: URL
if inMemory {
  url = URL(fileURLWithPath: "/dev/null")
} else {
  let groupName = "group.com.yourcompany.PushNotifications"
```

```
    url = FileManager.default
      .containerURL(forSecurityApplicationGroupIdentifier:
groupName)!
      .appendingPathComponent("PushNotifications.sqlite")
}

container.persistentStoreDescriptions.first!.url = url
```

You have to tell iOS exactly where to write the internal **.sqlite** file since the default doesn't work with app groups. Using the code shown allows you to identify exactly where Core Data should store the database. Be sure the group name you specify exactly matches what you specified for the App Group.

Remember to tell your service extension about this file. Bring up the **File inspector** by pressing ⌥ + ⌘ + 1 and in the **Target Membership** section check the box next to your service extension.

Localization

If you're modifying the content of your payload, you might be modifying the text as well. Always keep in mind that not everyone speaks the same language you do, so you still need to follow all the localization rules you normally would.

> **Note**: There's currently a bug in Xcode in which your base language will not always be used in an extension. To work around this bug, simply make sure that you have a **Localizable.strings** for your base language defined.

If the only reason you're using an extension is to perform localizations on text, you should instead look at the keys of the `aps alert` dictionary, as explained back in Chapter 3, "Remote Notification Payload", as there are multiple items there to perform this action for you.

Debugging

Sometimes, no matter how hard you try, things just don't go right. Debugging a service extension works almost the same as any other Xcode project. However, because it's a target and not an app, you have to take a few extra steps.

1. Open up your **NotificationService.swift** file and set a breakpoint on the line where you decode the title.
2. Build and run your app.
3. In Xcode's menu bar, choose **Debug ▸ Attach to Process by PID or Name...**.
4. In the dialog window that appears, enter **Payload Modification** — or whatever you named your target.
5. Press the **Attach** button.

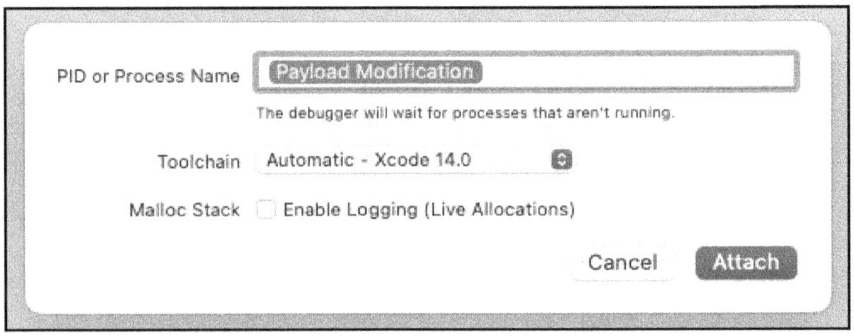

If you send yourself another push notification, Xcode should stop execution at the breakpoint you set. Be aware that debugging service extensions is a bit finicky and sometimes it just plain doesn't work. If you aren't able to find your process listed, you might have to go through a full restart of Xcode and possibly even a reboot of your device.

Key Points

- A Notification Service Extension is a sort of middleware between APNs and your UI. With it, you can receive a remote notification and modify its content before it's presented to the user.
- You may make any modification to the payload you want — except for one. You may not remove the alert text. If you don't have alert text, then iOS will ignore your modifications and proceed with the original payload.
- You can use service extensions to download videos or other content from the internet. Once downloaded, create a `UNNotificationAttachment` object that you attach to the push notification.
- Your primary app target and your extension are two separate processes and cannot share data between them by default. You can overcome this using App Groups.
- Service extensions can be used to handle your app's badge so that the badge reflects the number of unseen notifications without having to involve server side storage.
- You can access your app's data store in your extension once you have App Groups set up.
- When modifying the content of your payload, if your text is also changed, follow localization rules to account for different languages.

Chapter 11: Custom Interfaces

In the last few chapters, you worked through most types of notifications, including those that present an attachment, such as an image or video, alongside the banner message; but if you really want to go hog wild, you can even customize the way the notification itself looks to your heart's content! This can get quite complex, but it is worth the time to make an app that really shines. Custom interfaces are implemented as separate targets in your Xcode project, just like the service extension.

Your top-secret agency wants to send you the locations of your targets, so you'll need to build a way to do that. In this chapter, you'll create a notification that displays a location on the map, with the ability to comment on that location right from the notification, all without opening the app.

Configuring Xcode for a Custom Notification UI

After opening up the starter project for this chapter, set the team signing as discussed in Chapter 7, "Expanding the Application". Don't forget to also set the team signing for the **Payload Modification** target just as you did in the previous chapter, Chapter 10, "Modifying the Payload".

First, you'll create a new **Notification Content Extension** that will handle showing your custom UI.

1. In Xcode, select **File ▸ New ▸ Target...**.
2. Makes sure **iOS** is selected and choose the **Notification Content Extension.**
3. Press **Next.**
4. For the **Product Name** field type **Custom UI.**
5. Press **Finish.**
6. If asked about scheme activation, select **Cancel.**

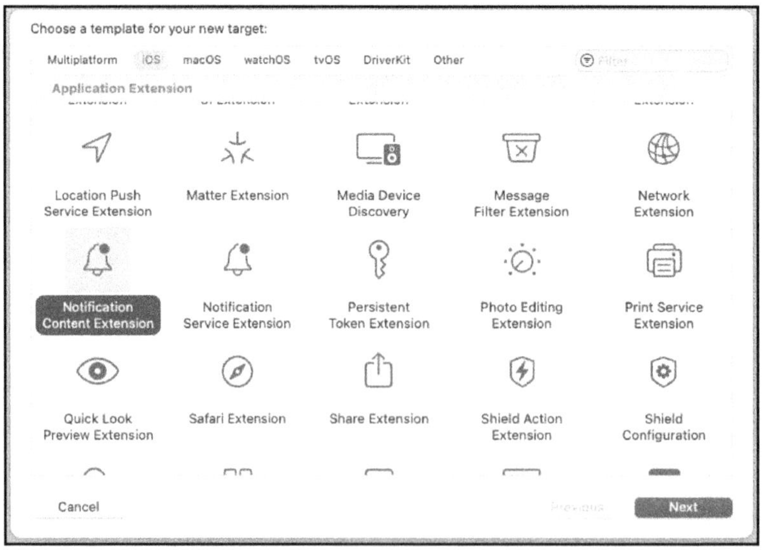

> **Note**: You don't actually *run* a **Notification Content Extension**, so that's why you didn't let it make the new target your active scheme.

You can name the new target anything that makes sense for you, but it can be helpful to use the above name because, when you glance at your project, you will immediately know what that target is doing.

Custom interfaces are triggered by specifying a category, just as you learned about with custom actions in Chapter 9, "Custom Actions".

Every custom UI must have its own unique category identifier. Bring up the Project navigator (⌘ + 1) and select your project. Then, select the newly created target and go to the **Info** tab. You'll see an item labeled **NSExtension**. Expand that *all the way* out and find a key labeled `UNNotificationExtensionCategory`. This identifier connects your main target, registering the identifier, with the correct content extension.

If your push notification contains a `category` key that matches this, the UI in your content extension will be used. Update this value to **ShowMap**.

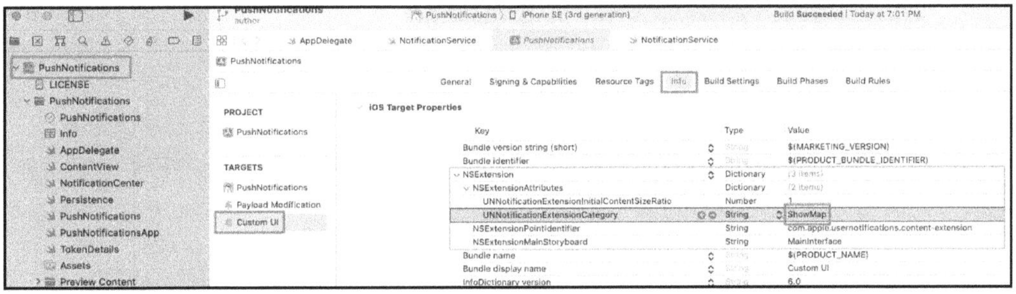

If you have multiple category types that will all use the same UI, simply change the type of `UNNotificationExtensionCategory` from `String` to `Array` and list each category name that you'd like to support.

Designing the Interface

You'll notice that your new target includes a storyboard and view controller for you to utilize. Wait...storyboard? But we want SwiftUI!

Go ahead and delete the **MainInterface.storyboard** file with extreme prejudice, then create a new SwiftUI View file called **MapView.swift** with the following contents:

```
import SwiftUI

struct MapView: View {
  let mapImage: Image
```

```
  var body: some View {
    mapImage
      .resizable()
      .aspectRatio(contentMode: .fit)
  }
}

struct MapView_Previews: PreviewProvider {
  static var previews: some View {
    MapView(mapImage: Image(systemName: "globe.americas"))
  }
}
```

> **Note**: There's currently a bug that prevents Xcode from displaying the preview in a content extension.

The view will display an image of the map location.

Decoding the Payload

When the notification arrives, you'll need to decode the payload to get the coordinates. You'll be working with `MapKit`, so in **NotificationViewController.swift**, add the follow two imports:

```
import CoreLocation
import MapKit
```

None of the code supplied by Xcode's template will be necessary, so you should remove the entire contents of the `NotificationViewController`'s implementation. Ignore the error saying that `NotificationViewController` does not conform to the `UNNotificationContentExtension` protocol. You'll fix that in just a bit.

When working with maps, you need to specify the region that will be displayed, so add a new property to `NotificationViewController`:

```
var region: MKCoordinateRegion!
```

Then, implement the following method:

```
private func decodeUserInfo(_ notification: UNNotification) {
  let userInfo = notification.request.content.userInfo

  guard
    let latitude = userInfo["latitude"] as? CLLocationDistance,
```

```
    let longitude = userInfo["longitude"] as?
CLLocationDistance,
    let radius = userInfo["radius"] as? CLLocationDistance
  else {
    // Default to Apple Park if nothing provided
    region = .init(
      center: .init(latitude: 37.334886, longitude:
-122.008988),
      span: .init(latitudeDelta: 0.2, longitudeDelta: 0.2)
    )

    return
  }

  let location = CLLocation(latitude: latitude, longitude:
longitude)
  region = .init(
    center: location.coordinate,
    latitudinalMeters: radius,
    longitudinalMeters: radius
  )
}
```

Your view controller has access to the full payload that was sent over by accessing the `userInfo` property of the `UNNotification` instance. You're simply pulling the `latitude`, `longitude` and `radius` from your payload, constructing the appropriate `CoreLocation` objects, and then returning an `MKCoordinateRegion` that your map will display.

To keep the sample code simple, if anything is missing, or fails to convert property, the app defaults to showing Apple Park's coordinates. A production app would likely have more logic in the `MapView` to show something different with a message saying there was a problem with the coordinates.

Adding a UIHostingController

A custom UI for a push notification is required to use UIKit and a `UIViewController`. However, with a bit of magic, you can still utilize SwiftUI for the display. You'll implement what's known as a Container View Controller (https://apple.co/3BsAQna). Essentially you take a view controller and make it a child of another view controller.

Apple has provided the `UIHostingController` class to support using SwiftUI views inside of a UIKit framework. By making the hosting controller a child of the custom UI's view controller, you now have a way to show your SwiftUI view in a custom push notification.

Replace the import of `UIKit` with `SwiftUI`, then add a `UIHostingController` property to the class:

```
var mapViewHost: UIHostingController<MapView>!
```

The `mapViewHost` property is the UIKit enabled wrapper for your SwiftUI `MapView`.

Receiving the Notification

When a notification arrives, iOS will call the `didReceive(_:)` method. Replace the contents of the method with the following:

```
// 1
decodeUserInfo(notification)

// 2
let mapView = MapView(mapImage: Image(systemName:
"globe.americas"))
mapViewHost = UIHostingController(rootView: mapView)

// 3
addChild(mapViewHost)
view.addSubview(mapViewHost.view)

// 4
mapViewHost.view.translatesAutoresizingMaskIntoConstraints =
false

NSLayoutConstraint.activate([
  mapViewHost.view.topAnchor.constraint(equalTo:
view.topAnchor),
  mapViewHost.view.bottomAnchor.constraint(equalTo:
view.bottomAnchor),
  mapViewHost.view.leadingAnchor.constraint(equalTo:
view.leadingAnchor),
  mapViewHost.view.trailingAnchor.constraint(equalTo:
view.trailingAnchor)
])

// 5
mapViewHost.didMove(toParent: self)
```

In the preceding code:

1. You first decode the payload that was sent via the notification.
2. Next, you create a `UIHostingController` that wraps your SwiftUI view. This is your child view controller.

3. Add the hosting controller as a child of the current controller and add the map's root view as a child of the current view.
4. It's important to tell iOS not to add any constraints as you're going to handle them yourself. Specify that the map's view should take up the entire view, regardless of size.
5. Finally, tell the child controller that it has moved to its parent.

With that simple trick, you've ensured that every time a remote push notification is received, iOS will create a new SwiftUI view and attach it to the normal `UIViewController` that you're still required to use.

> **Note**: `loadView` is called *before* `didReceive(_:)`. Do not attempt to create the `MapView` outside of the `didReceive(_:)` method.

The previous code is forcing a globe to always be shown, which isn't very useful. You're probably wondering why the `MapView` doesn't use the actual `MapKit` framework. Unfortunately, the map in iOS 16 is very memory intensive. If you try to use it in a custom interface, your notification will crash due to memory overload.

> **Note**: Apple is aware of the issue and is researching a fix, as of iOS 16 Beta 4.

MKMapSnapshotter

The solution is to use an `MKMapSnapshotter`. Given an `MKCoordinateRegion`, iOS will take a picture of the map for that region and provide it to your code as a UIImage. There are two methods you can use:

- `start(with:completionHandler:)`
- `start(with:) async throws`

While you would normally prefer the second method, iOS does not yet allow for an `async` version of `didRecieve(_:)`. The first version is equally problematic due to the completion handler. All of your work must be completed *before* leaving the `didReceive(_:)` method.

This is one of the rare cases where you'll need to explicitly block the thread and wait for a task to complete. By utilizing a `DispatchGroup` you can call the method taking a completion handler, then block progress until the completion handler completes.

Replace the `MapView` creation line with the following:

```
// 1
var mapImage = Image(systemName: "globe.americas")

// 2
let group = DispatchGroup()
group.enter()

// 3
let options = MKMapSnapshotter.Options()
options.region = region

let snapshotter = MKMapSnapshotter(options: options)

// 4
snapshotter.start(with: .global(qos: .userInitiated))
{ (snapshot, _) in
  // 5
  if let image = snapshot?.image {
    mapImage = Image(uiImage: image)
  }

  // 6
  group.leave()
}

// 7
group.wait()

// 8
let mapView = MapView(mapImage: mapImage)
```

If you aren't familiar with iOS concurrency programming, check out *Concurrency by Tutorials (*https://bit.ly/3QEllgc*)* from our professional subscription package. Here's what's happening:

1. It's always possible something could go wrong, bad coordinates were given, etc... You'll default to showing a globe if that happens.
2. Entering a `DispatchGroup` tells iOS to start keeping track of which groups have started and completed.
3. You're initializing an `MKMapSnapshotter` for the region specified in the payload.
4. The `start(with:completionHandler:)` tells iOS to generate a map at the given region and then, once it's done so, to call the completion handler with the image of that map. You want the action to run as fast as possible, so you're specifying the `.userInitiated` quality of service.

5. If iOS successfully create a snapshot image, you replace the default globe with the snapshot.
6. Calling `leave` lets iOS know that this group has completed.
7. The `wait` method forces iOS to stop execution at this point until every call to `enter` has had a corresponding `leave` call. If you `enter` 5 groups, you must `leave` 5 groups before `wait` will move on.
8. Finally, you now create the `MapView` with the snapshotted image.

Forcing iOS to block and wait is always a bad idea if there's any other option. Unfortunately, this is a case where you have no choice.

If you were to build and run your app, the custom UI wouldn't display.

Setting the Entry Point

Remember that the default template expects to display a storyboard. Edit the **Info.plist** file, the expand the `NSExtension` key. You will see a key labeled `NSExtensionMainStoryboard`. Replace the key with `NSExtensionPrincipalClass`, then replace the value with `$(PRODUCT_MODULE_NAME).NotificationViewController`. Using the `NSExtensionPrincipalClass` key lets iOS know how to start your custom UI as you no longer have a storyboard to load.

Build and run your app so that you can test everything. There shouldn't be any warnings or errors from the build. If you haven't set up your **PushNotifications** tester app, do so now as described in Chapter 5, "Sending Your First Push Notification". Make sure you change your payload to the following JSON:

```
{
  "aps": {
    "alert" : {
      "title" : "The Sydney Observatory"
    },
    "category" : "ShowMap",
    "sound": "default"
  },
  "latitude" : -33.859574,
  "longitude" : 151.204576,
  "radius" : 500
}
```

Now, send the push notification. You should see a notification come in and, by long-pressing it, you should see the location on a map right inside the notification!

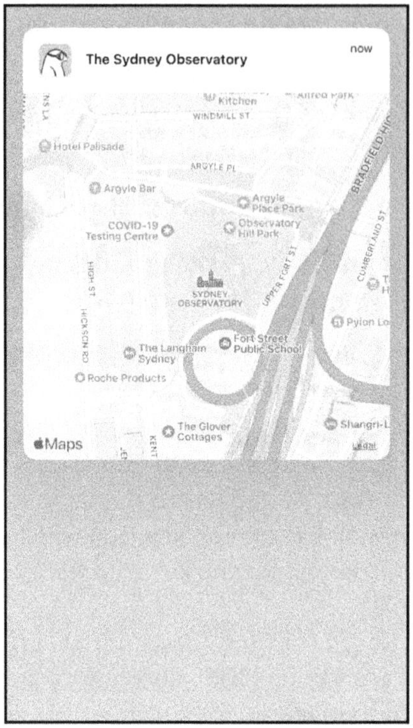

You'll quickly notice, if you try to pan or zoom the map, the custom UI view controller, while fully functional, does not accept any type of user input. Keep this in mind while designing your interface. In a map example, it probably doesn't make sense to place any pins on the view as the end user won't be able to touch them to get more information, which could lead to confusion.

Also keep in mind that your custom interface is still just an iOS target. This means that you can easily share properly encapsulated `UIView`s between your main target and the content extension. Just add the `UIView` to the content extension target in the **File Inspector** (⌥ + ⌘ + 1), and you can use it like any other view! You can refer back to Chapter 10, "Modifying the Payload", in which you added the **UserDefaults.swift** file to the service extension, if you need a reminder of how this works.

> **Note**: There is an issue in the iOS 16 beta where the map view sometimes causes the notification UI to crash and display a plain white view. Apple has told us they are working on a fix, but for now you can send yourself another notification in case the first one crashes.

Resizing the Initial View

If you watch really closely while your custom UI comes into place, you'll probably notice that it might start a bit too big and then shrink down to the proper size. Apple, without explaining why, implemented the initial height of the view as a percentage of the width, instead of letting you specify a specific size.

In the **Info.plist** of your target extension, you can expand the **NSExtension** row again, where you'll see a setting for `UNNotificationExtensionInitialContentSizeRatio`, which defaults to `1`. You should set this to a decimal value less than or equal to `1`, representing the ratio of the height to the width. If you specify `0.8`, for example, the UI will start with a height that is `80%` as tall as the width. Trial and error are your friend in getting this just right.

Accepting Text Input

At times, you may want to allow your users to type some text in response to a push notification. With the previous map push, people may want to tell you how jealous they are that you're there or the awesome things they saw last time they went themselves. Or, in your spy app, you might want to request additional information about your target.

Head over to the **PushNotifications.swift** file. First, add the following `enum` inside of the `PushNotifications` enum:

```
private enum ActionIdentifier: String {
  case comment
}
```

Even though it's just a single action, you should still use an `enum` so that additions are easier in the future with less code refactoring.

You'll need to create your `registerCustomActions()` method to include an action button. This time, though, you'll use the `UNTextInputNotificationAction` type. Still inside the `PushNotifications` enum, add the following code:

```
private static let categoryIdentifier = "ShowMap"

static func registerCustomActions() {
  let ident = ActionIdentifier.comment.rawValue
  let comment = UNTextInputNotificationAction(
    identifier: ident,
    title: "Comment"
  )

  let category = UNNotificationCategory(
    identifier: categoryIdentifier,
    actions: [comment],
    intentIdentifiers: []
  )

UNUserNotificationCenter.current().setNotificationCategories([ca
tegory])
}
```

Note that you're asking for *text* input instead of a button click, so be sure you use the `UNTextInputNotificationAction` action type.

Finally, call your new method at the end of `application(_:didRegisterForRemoteNotificationsWithDeviceToken:)` in **AppDelegate.swift**:

```
PushNotifications.registerCustomActions()
```

If you build and run the app, then send that same push notification to yourself again, you should now have a keyboard on screen!

> **Note**: Remember that custom actions won't work in the simulator, so you'll need to run on a physical device.

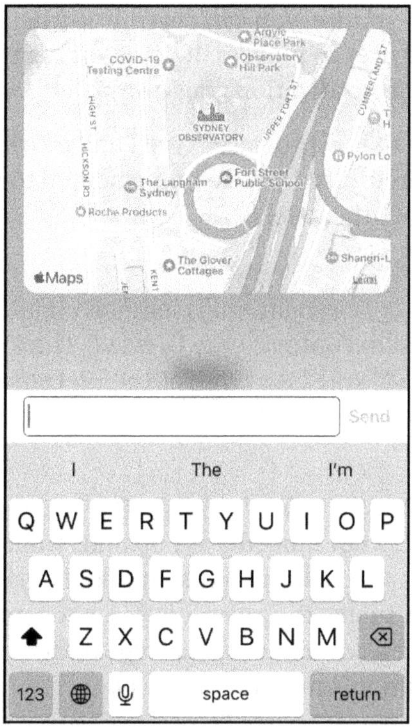

You'll notice that you received a keyboard directly and not a **Comment** button. iOS is smart enough to realize that, if your only action is a keyboard action, it should just show the keyboard by default. If you were to add another action, however, you'd instead get an actual button labeled **Comment** that you'd tap to open the keyboard.

Showing a keyboard is great, but now you've got to know what was said! To get the text that was typed by the user, you must implement a new delegate method in your Content UI extension. In **NotificationViewController.swift**, add:

```
func didReceive(
  _ response: UNNotificationResponse
) async -> UNNotificationContentExtensionResponseOption {
  guard let response = response as?
UNTextInputNotificationResponse else {
    return .dismiss
  }

  let text = response.userText

  // Process the text as appropriate.

  return .dismiss
}
```

By looking at the type of response, you can determine whether or not you've received text from the end user to process. If you didn't get text, then simply return `.dismiss` so that the notification goes away.

All that's left to do is grab the text the user typed and process it. Frequently, this will mean calling some web service that you've implemented to store the response and possibly send it back out to other users.

> **Note**: The `didReceive(_:)` synchronous method is called when the notification is displayed to configure the UI itself. The `didReceive(_:)` async method, that returns a `UNNotificationContentExtensionResponseOption`, is called in response to tapping an action button or by pressing **Send** on the keyboard.

When using a custom UI, it's not immediately obvious what to do with the notification after you've tapped a button or sent text. Is that it? Should iOS now dismiss the notification? Usually, the answer is yes, but sometimes you'll want to send text *and* be able to hit a social media *like*-type button. In the latter case, you wouldn't want the notification window to go away.

If multiple interactions with your UI are possible, you'd instead want to return `.doNotDismiss`.

There is a third, not normally used, possibility. You can specify `.dismissAndForwardAction` to simply dismiss the custom UI and send the notification straight to your main app.

Changing Actions

It's also possible to modify the action buttons dynamically inside of your Notification Content Extension. If you're sending a social media notification, for example, you may want to provide a button to let the end-user "like" your content. Once you've tapped the "Like" button, it only makes sense to now provide an "Unlike" button in its place. In the case of your spy app, you'll add "Accept" and "Cancel" buttons, to accept your next target and cancel the mission if anything goes wrong.

By simply modifying the `notificationActions` property on the `extensionContext` variable you can do just that!

First, in **NotificationViewController.swift**, add the following `enum` to the top of the class:

```
enum ActionIdentifier: String {
  case accept
  case cancel
}
```

These are identifiers for your **Accept** and **Cancel** actions. Next, update the *asynchronous* `didReceive(_:)` with the following code:

```
func didReceive(
  _ response: UNNotificationResponse
) async -> UNNotificationContentExtensionResponseOption {
  let accept = ActionIdentifier.accept.rawValue
  let cancel = ActionIdentifier.cancel.rawValue
  let currentActions = extensionContext?.notificationActions ??
[]

  switch response.actionIdentifier {
  case accept:
    let cancel = UNNotificationAction(identifier: cancel, title:
"Cancel")
    extensionContext?.notificationActions = currentActions
      .map { $0.identifier == accept ? cancel : $0 }

  case cancel:
    let accept = UNNotificationAction(identifier: accept, title:
"Accept")
    extensionContext?.notificationActions = currentActions
      .map { $0.identifier == cancel ? accept : $0 }

  default:
    break
  }

  return .doNotDismiss
}
```

The `actionIdentifier` property inside the notification response tells you which button was tapped. If the user tapped the **Accept** button, you'll create a **Cancel** button and replace the existing **Accept** button with it. Similarly, if the user tapped the **Cancel** button, you'll replace it with the **Accept** button. You'll make these changes by modifying the `notificationActions` property of the content extension's context.

While you could make this a tiny bit easier to read by simply replacing the index of the button directly, as opposed to using the `map`, this is definitely much more future-proof. This way, you don't have to worry if you decide to add new buttons that change the order of your actions.

Still in **NotificationViewController.swift**, add the following lines to the bottom of the `didReceive(_:)` *synchronous* method:

```
let acceptAction = UNNotificationAction(
  identifier: ActionIdentifier.accept.rawValue,
  title: "Accept")
extensionContext?.notificationActions = [acceptAction]
```

This will make sure the **Accept** action shows up when you receive a notification.

Finally, you have to remove the comment action. Head to **PushNotifications.swift** and modify the contents of the `registerCustomActions` method to the following:

```
let category = UNNotificationCategory(
  identifier: categoryIdentifier,
  actions: [],
  intentIdentifiers: [])

UNUserNotificationCenter.current().setNotificationCategories([ca
tegory])
```

Since you're setting the actions inside the UI extension, there's no need to call `registerCustomActions` in **AppDelegate.swift**, so remove the call.

Build and run your app. You should see an **Accept** button on the notification and, when you tap it, it should change into a **Cancel** button.

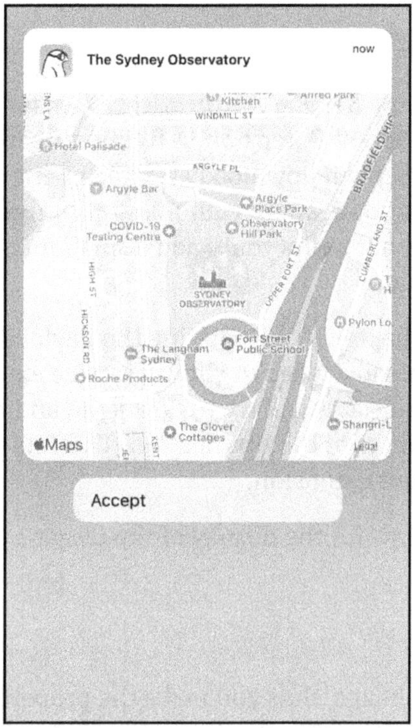

> **Note**: iOS will sometimes cache your content extension and it will stay the same between builds even though you changed your code. If that happens, delete the app from your device and rebuild the project from Xcode. Note that this might change your device token used for sending notifications.

By using this in conjunction with modifying the custom UI in response to tapping on an action button, you can now present a very rich user experience.

The fact that Apple now makes the action buttons dynamic also means that you're no longer required to set up all of your actions when you register your category. You might, for example, simply register the category to trigger the extension and then dynamically generate all of your buttons based on the content of the payload, which provides major flexibility benefits.

You're also able to present layered actions, but you need to again think very carefully about your user experience doing this. For example, the "Like" button may replace all the existing buttons with something like Love, Like, Kind of Like, and Meh. However, just because you *can* do something doesn't mean that you *should* do something!

Attachments

If your project also includes a Service Notification Extension, it will be executed *before* your Notification Content Extension. A frequent reason you'd have both extensions is that the former will download an attachment that the latter wants to use. It's not enough to just know where your mission's target is. You also need to know what they look like; that's why you'll add a small image of your target's headshot to your notification.

In the previous chapter, Chapter 10, "Modifying the Payload", you used a notification service extension to download a video. A similar service extension is already included in your starter project. It will try to download an image and a video, and then add them as attachments to the notification. This lets you use those attachments in your content extension.

Edit **MapView.swift** to allow for the display of the target's picture by adding the following property:

```
let targetImage: Image?
```

You won't always have an image, thus you make the property optional. To display the image, add the following code right after the `aspectRatio(contentMode: .fit)` line:

```
.overlay(alignment: .topTrailing) {
  if let targetImage {
    targetImage
      .resizable()
      .aspectRatio(contentMode: .fit)
      .frame(width: 80.0, height: 80.0)
  }
}
```

If the image is present, it will appear as an 80x80 picture at the top of the map, on the trailing edge.

You'll also need to update the `PreviewProvider` to pass a `nil` to the constructor:

```
struct MapView_Previews: PreviewProvider {
  static var previews: some View {
    MapView(mapImage: Image(systemName: "globe.americas"),
targetImage: nil)
  }
}
```

In **NotificationViewController.swift**, add the following method:

```
private func getImage(_ notification: UNNotification) -> Image?
{
  // 1
  guard
    let attachment =
notification.request.content.attachments.first,
    attachment.url.startAccessingSecurityScopedResource()
  else {
    return nil
  }
  // 2
  defer { attachment.url.stopAccessingSecurityScopedResource() }
  // 3
  guard
    let data = try? Data(contentsOf: attachment.url),
    let uimage = UIImage(data: data)
  else {
    return nil
  }

  return Image(uiImage: uimage)
}
```

Getting the image requires a couple steps:

1. Due to the way iOS performs its sandboxing, for security reasons, you can't just directly access the attachment. You must first access the scoped resource.
2. You'll want to stop accessing the resource regardless of how you exit the method.
3. If you're not able to download and decode a valid image, then just return `nil`.
4. If everything worked, generate a new SwiftUI `Image`.

All that's left to do is update the `MapView` creation to pass the image:

```
let mapView = MapView(region: region, image:
getImage(notification))
```

Build and run the app. In the push notification tester app, update the payload to the following JSON. It now includes the `mutable-content` key, so that the payload modification target runs, and the `media-url`, that points to your target's image:

```
{
  "aps": {
    "alert" : {
      "title" : "The Sydney Observatory"
    },
```

```
    "category" : "ShowMap",
    "sound": "default",
    "mutable-content": 1
  },
  "latitude" : -33.859574,
  "longitude" : 151.204576,
  "radius" : 500,
  "media-url": "https://www.gravatar.com/avatar/
8477f7be4418a0ce325b2b41e5298e4c.jpg"
}
```

Send the push notification. You should see an attached image on the notification and, when you press into it, you should see an image of your next target:

> **Note**: The image frequently fails to display properly in the simulator, so test on a real device.

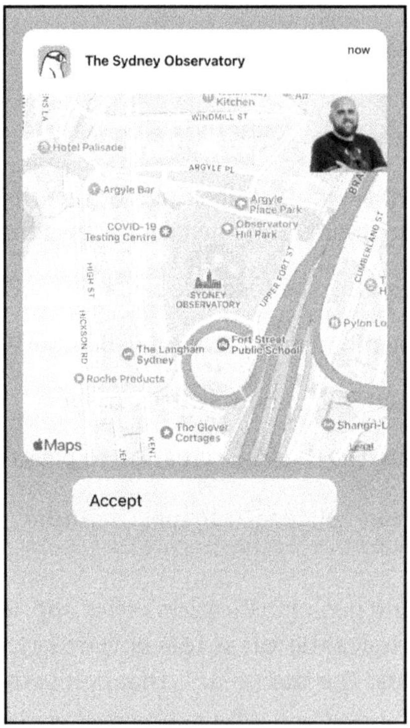

Whoa! Looks like Shai is in for some big trouble.

Video Attachments

Things get more complicated when your attachment is a video file, however. While this is out-of-scope for your spy app, it's still a valuable feature to know about.

As you remember, custom UI notifications are *not* interactive by default, meaning you can't simply tap on a media player to start and stop the video like you normally would.

If you have a video player as part of your custom notification UI, you'll need to implement at least two of the three optional delegate properties:

```
// 1
var mediaPlayPauseButtonType:
  UNNotificationContentExtensionMediaPlayPauseButtonType {
  return .overlay
}

// 2
var mediaPlayPauseButtonFrame: CGRect {
  return CGRect(x: 0, y: 0, width: 44, height: 44)
}

// 3
var mediaPlayPauseButtonTintColor: UIColor {
  return .purple
}
```

Here's what these lines of code are for:

1. You ask iOS to draw a button that either disappears on play (`.overlay`) or stays onscreen (`.default`).
2. You must tell iOS exactly what `CGRect` to use for positioning and sizing the **Play** button.
3. Optionally, you can specify the tinting of the button to match your theme.

The button iOS draws for you will be tappable. When tapped, the `UNNotificationContentExtension` delegate methods `mediaPlay` and `mediaPause` will be called so that you can take action on your video player controller.

Custom User Input

While action buttons and the keyboard are great, sometimes you really just want your own custom interface for user input – a grid of buttons, sliders, etc...

> **Note**: If you provide a custom input, you can't also have an option for the keyboard to appear. You need to pick one or the other.

Adding a Payment Action

Agents need to get paid! You'll add a slider that the agents can use to select how much they want to get paid for the job. Head back into your app's **PushNotifications.swift** file and add a new case to the `ActionIdentifier` enum:

```
case payment
```

Next, replace the contents of `registerCustomActions` with the following:

```
let identifier = ActionIdentifier.payment.rawValue
let payment = UNNotificationAction(
  identifier: identifier,
  title: "Payment")

let category = UNNotificationCategory(
  identifier: categoryIdentifier,
  actions: [payment],
  intentIdentifiers: [])

UNUserNotificationCenter.current().setNotificationCategories([ca
tegory])
```

Here, you set the new action as a category on the notification, as you did before.

Next, in **NotificationViewController.swift**, delete the following lines from `didReceive(_:)`:

```
let acceptAction = UNNotificationAction(
  identifier: ActionIdentifier.accept.rawValue,
  title: "Accept")
extensionContext!.notificationActions = [acceptAction]
```

Finally, add a call to `registerCustomActions` back to the end of `application(_:didRegisterForRemoteNotificationsWithDeviceToken)` in **AppDelegate.swift**:

```
PushNotifications.registerCustomActions()
```

This will make sure the new payment action shows up below the notification.

The First Responder

Remember way back when you first learned iOS programming, there was that pesky responder chain that never made much sense? Well, it's finally time to do something useful with it!

Still in **NotificationViewController.swift**, add an override to the top of the class to tell the system that you can, in fact, become the first responder:

```
override var canBecomeFirstResponder: Bool {
  return true
}
```

When the user taps on your **Payment** button, you want to become the first responder so that you can present a custom user interaction view. Replace the contents of the asynchronous `didReceive(_:)` with the following to make that happen:

```
_ = becomeFirstResponder()
return .doNotDismiss
```

The User Input

If you become the first responder, iOS will expect you to return a view via the `inputView` property that contains your custom user interaction view. The download materials for this chapter includes a `PaymentView` for you that will display a slider for selecting payments. Drag the **PaymentView.swift** file from the projects folder into the **Custom UI** group in **Xcode**. Make sure **Copy items if needed** is checked, and also that the **Custom UI** target is checked.

Back in **NotificationViewController.swift**, add the following properties to the top of the class to tell the system to use your new view:

```
private lazy var paymentView: PaymentView = {
  let paymentView = PaymentView()
  paymentView.onPaymentRequested = { [weak self] payment in
    self?.resignFirstResponder()
  }
  return paymentView
}()

override var inputView: UIView? {
  return paymentView
}
```

When the view controller becomes the first responder, iOS will ask it for the input view to display. Build and run the app and send yourself another push notification.

After tapping on the **Payment** button, you'll see a slider to select your payment:

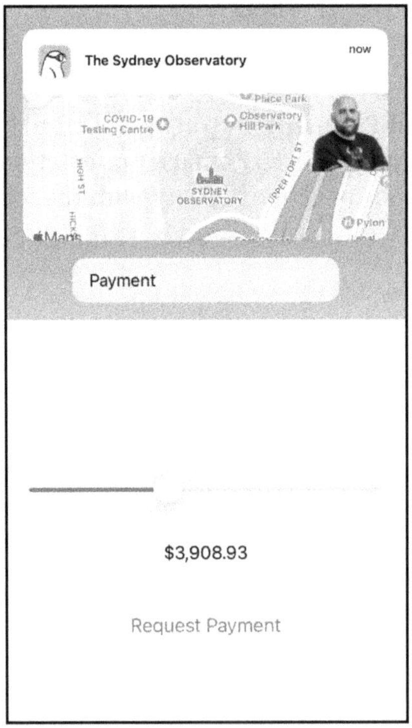

Hiding Default Content

If you're creating a custom UI, odds are that you're already presenting the title and body of the notification somewhere in your UI. If that's the case, you can tell iOS to not present that default data under your view by editing the content extension's **Info.plist**. Expand the **NSExtension** property again. This time, under **NSExtensionAttributes**, add a new `Boolean` key called `UNNotificationExtensionDefaultContentHidden` and set its value to `YES`.

Key	Type	Value
∨ NSExtension	Dictionary	(3 items)
∨ NSExtensionAttributes	Dictionary	(3 items)
UNNotificationExtensionDefaultContentHidden	Boolean	1
UNNotificationExtensionCategory	String	ShowMap
UNNotificationExtensionInitialContentSizeRatio	Number	1

Delivering a notification with this setting will show the same custom UI, without the title text:

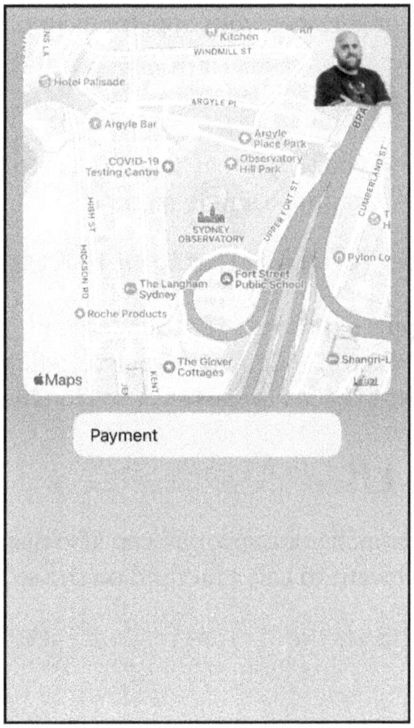

Interactive UI

If you want to support interactive touches on your custom user interface, you need to edit the **Info.plist** of your extension and add the `UNNotificationExtensionUserInteractionEnabled` attribute key with a value of `YES` inside `NSExtensionAttributes`.

Key	Type	Value
NSExtension	Dictionary	(3 items)
NSExtensionAttributes	Dictionary	(4 items)
UNNotificationExtensionUserInteractionEnabled	Boolean	1
UNNotificationExtensionDefaultContentHidden	Boolean	1
UNNotificationExtensionCategory	String	ShowMap
UNNotificationExtensionInitialContentSizeRatio	Number	1

At this point, you can create an `IBOutlet` like you would on a normal view controller and link appropriate actions to them. It's important to remember that you are responsible for handling all of the actions and callbacks once you've done this. Tapping on the UI will no longer open your app, for example.

Launching the App

Depending on the content of your UI, it may make sense to have a button tap launch your app. This is as simple as calling a single method:

```
extensionContext?.performNotificationDefaultAction()
```

Once that's called, your app's `userNotificationCenter(_:didReceive:)` delegate method, from `UNUserNotificationCenterDelegate`, will be called, and the identifier will be set to `UNNotificationDefaultActionIdentifier`.

Dismissing the UI

Similarly to being able to launch your app, you can also dismiss the UI based on a button tap. As usual, you'll want to call a method on the `extensionContext`:

```
extensionContext?.dismissNotificationContentExtension()
```

Debugging

Debugging a UI extension works almost the same as any other Xcode project. However, because it's a target and not an app, you have to take a few extra steps.

1. Open up your **NotificationViewController.swift** file and set a breakpoint where you need to start debugging.
2. Build and run your app.
3. In Xcode's menu bar choose **Debug ▸ Attach to Process by PID or Name....**
4. In the dialog window that appears, enter **Custom UI**, or whatever you named your target.
5. Press the **Attach** button.

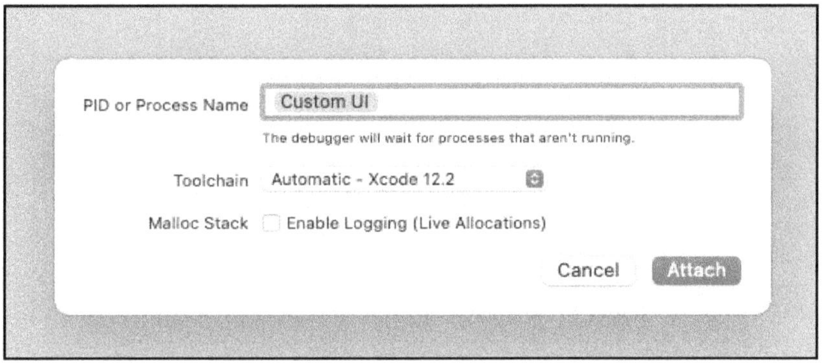

If you switch over to the **Debug Navigator** (⌘ + 7) you'll see that Xcode is waiting for your target to start before it can attach to it.

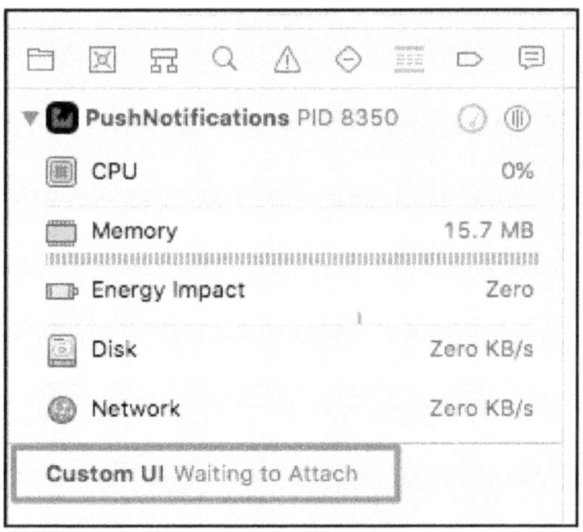

If you send yourself another push and open up the custom UI, Xcode will show that it's attached to your process.

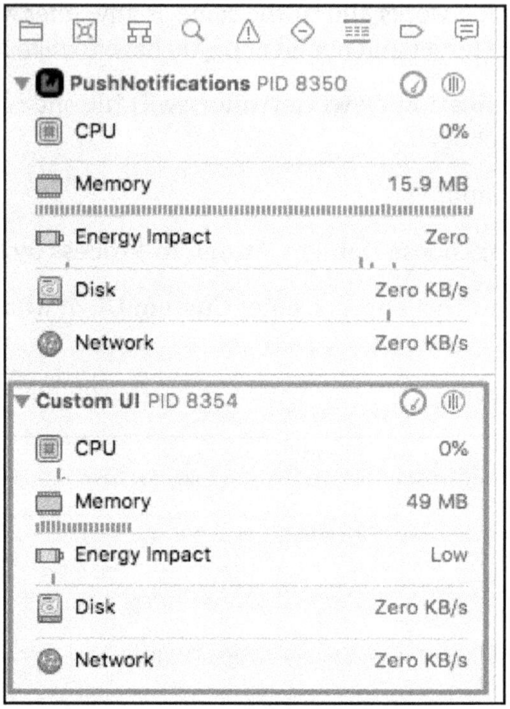

It's important to point this out as you need to wait for the process to be attached before you interact with your user interface beyond the initial long-press to open the UI. If you tap on anything before Xcode has attached, you won't actually hit your breakpoint.

Print With Breakpoints

Because your custom interface runs as a separate process, you will not see any `print` statements that you place in your code. Instead, you'll need to make use of Xcode breakpoints.

Set a breakpoint like you normally would, right-click on the breakpoint and choose **Edit Breakpoint...**.

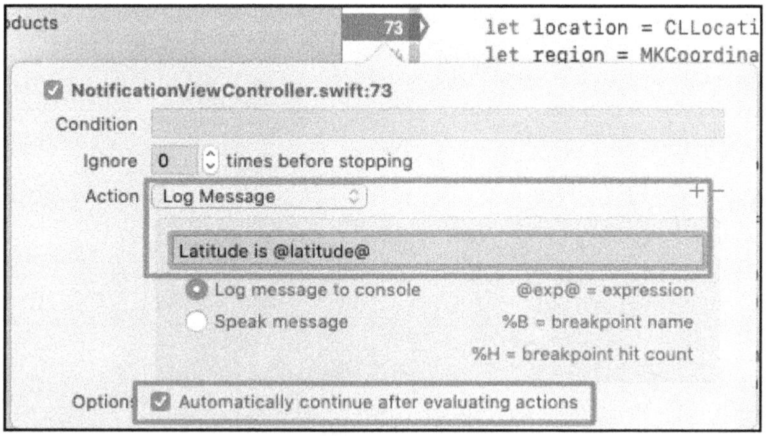

Set the **Action** dropdown to **Log Message**. You can surround variable names with `@` symbols to display the value of a variable. The message you display will appear in the Xcode console.

Be sure that you also select to **Automatically continue after evaluating actions** so that your app doesn't stop at the breakpoint.

Key Points

- You can customize the look of a push notification; custom interfaces are implemented as separate targets in your Xcode project, just like the service extension.
- Custom interfaces are triggered by specifying a category and every custom UI must have its own unique category identifier.
- There are a number of customizations you can make such as allowing your user to respond to a push notification with text, changing action buttons, allowing attachements and tailoring your interface for user input like payment actions. You can also hide default content and create an interactive UI. All of these features will enhance your user experience and make your app really stand out.

Chapter 12: Putting It All Together

With 11 chapters behind you, you've become quite the master of everything related to Push Notifications!

This chapter is all about leveraging all that you've learned in this book into a single app, titled **CoolCalendar**.

When somebody sends you a calendar invite, it will be pushed to your device via a remote notification. You'll have the ability to see how the new event relates to your existing calendars, be able to accept/reject right from the notification and have the option of sending a comment back.

Setting up the Xcode Project

Open this chapter's materials and you'll see a starter project called **CoolCalendar** prepared with the setup you've learned throughout this book. Here's what the starter project already includes:

1. The **Push Notifications** capability as discussed in Chapter 4, "Xcode Project Setup".
2. The **Remote notifications** as part of **Background Modes** as discussed in Chapter 8, "Handling Common Scenarios".
3. An **AppDelegate.swift** file as discussed in Chapter 4, "Xcode Project Setup".
4. **NotificationCenter.swift**, **PushNotifications.swift** and **TokenDetails.swift** files, as discussed in Chapter 8, "Handling Common Scenarios".
5. A **Notification Service Extension**, called Payload Modification, as discussed in Chapter 10, "Modifying the Payload".
6. A **Notification Content Extension**, called Custom UI, as discussed in Chapter 11, "Custom Interfaces".
7. A Core Data model called **Invite** representing a calendar invitation.
8. A **NotificationViewController.swift** file which includes helpers to display CalendarKit views in a notification.
9. A Swift package called CalendarKit.

The starter saves you from a bunch of boilerplate so you can hit the ground running.

AppDelegate Code Challenge

Take a minute to set up your `AppDelegate` code the way you think it should be. Keep in mind all the items discussed in the preceding chapters and don't be afraid to flip back to one or more for help!

Some features that you'll want to be sure to handle:

- You'll need action identifiers to know which custom action buttons were selected. Plan to have buttons for **Accept**, **Decline** and **Comment**.
- You'll need to register all of your custom actions.

- You'll need to register for push notifications.
- The payload's custom category will be called `CalendarInvite`.

Try to do this yourself. When you're ready, read the section below to find one potential solution. Don't peek until you've tried it yourself!

One Potential Solution

Start by creating a new file called **ActionIdentifier.swift** in your main **CoolCalendar** target, but make sure the **Custom UI** target is checked as well when you're creating the file. Add the following `enum` to the file:

```
enum ActionIdentifier: String {
  case accept
  case decline
  case comment
}
```

This defines your Action Identifiers.

Next, add your custom actions to **AppDelegate.swift** by adding the following code inside the class:

```
private let categoryIdentifier = "CalendarInvite"

private func registerCustomActions() {
  let accept = UNNotificationAction(
    identifier: ActionIdentifier.accept.rawValue,
    title: "Accept")

  let decline = UNNotificationAction(
    identifier: ActionIdentifier.decline.rawValue,
    title: "Decline")

  let comment = UNTextInputNotificationAction(
    identifier: ActionIdentifier.comment.rawValue,
    title: "Comment",
    options: [])

  let category = UNNotificationCategory(
    identifier: categoryIdentifier,
    actions: [accept, decline, comment],
    intentIdentifiers: [])

  UNUserNotificationCenter
    .current()
    .setNotificationCategories([category])
}
```

Then call that method from the end of
`application(_:didRegisterForRemoteNotificationsWithDeviceToken:)`

```
registerCustomActions()
```

If you build your app, it should compile cleanly at this point. Be sure not to move on until you are left with no compiler errors.

Requesting Calendar Permissions

Accessing the user's calendar is a privacy concern, and so you'll have to first request permission of your end users. Apple kindly ensured that the same authorization status is shared by all targets of your app.

This means that your extensions can simply look at the status and not have to ask for it, as the primary target already takes care of that. Like all good iOS apps, you'll have to tell your end users *why* you want to get into their calendars, so go back to the **CoolCalendar** target's **Info** panel and add a **Privacy — Calendars Usage Description** key.

You can use any text that explains why you need access to the Calendar, such as, "We need access to the Calendar to import your events and important dates."

Now, edit **ContentView** and request permission to the user's calendar when the view appears. This is boilerplate code that you'll use in any calendar app, but it's important to get it right.

First, you'll need to tell Xcode you're going to work with events by adding an import statement to the top of the file:

```
import EventKit
```

The event store is the way your app will communicate with the calendar data so add a property for it to the top of the `struct`:

```
@State private var eventStore = EKEventStore()
```

You'll need to track whether or not an alert should appear asking for permissions so add some state for that just above where you set the `eventStore`:

```
@State private var askForCalendarPermissions = false
```

Whenever the view appears you need to ensure that calendar permissions are still granted. If they're not, you should flag that you need to ask for those permissions. Add an `onAppear` method to the ContentView `struct`:

```
func onAppear() {
  let status = EKEventStore.authorizationStatus(for: .event)
  switch status {
  case .notDetermined:
    Task {
      askForCalendarPermissions = try! await
eventStore.requestAccess(to: .event)
    }
  case .authorized:
    break
  default:
    askForCalendarPermissions = true
  }
}
```

If access has to be requested, then you'll want to display an action sheet requesting the user grant you those rights. Right after `onAppear`, add a method to configure the `ActionSheet` which will appear.

```
func actionSheet() -> ActionSheet {
  ActionSheet(
    title: Text("This application requires calendar access"),
    message: Text("Grant access?"),
    buttons: [
      .default(Text("Settings")) {
        let str = UIApplication.openSettingsURLString
        UIApplication.shared.open(URL(string: str)!)
      },
      .cancel()
    ])
}
```

Finally, wire those two methods up to the body for your view. Your body should look like this now:

```
var body: some View {
  Text("Hello")
    .onAppear(perform: onAppear)
    .actionSheet(isPresented: $askForCalendarPermissions,
content: actionSheet)
}
```

While you could have placed those two methods inline with the body, separating the functionality into methods keeps the code cleaner and easier to test.

If you're not familiar with SwiftUI, that all probably looks like magic. Because `askForCalendarPermissions` was marked as `@State`, the view knows that it controls that variable and it can **bind** to it. The `$` in front of the variable name tells the action sheet that it should be presented when the value is true. Because it's a binding, the check is constantly performed. Thus, as soon as you set the value to `true`, the action sheet will appear.

> **Note**: It's a nice touch to give the user a simple way to get to your app settings, if permissions aren't currently granted.
>
> However, you should be sure *where* you're doing this from. In the case of this app, it's done every time the view appears if permission has been denied or not yet requested.
>
> If your app *requires* calendar access, this makes sense. However, if it's optional, and not 100% necessary to your app's functionality, then you'll just annoy the end user if you ask every single time.

Build and run the app to verify that you're asked to grant calendar permissions and to allow push notifications.

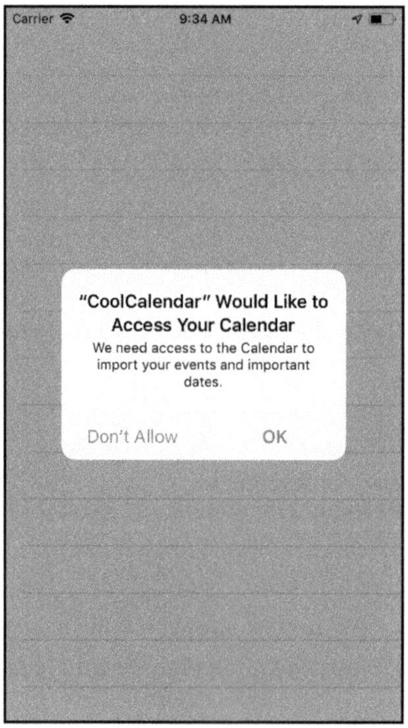

Be sure to tap **OK** on both! If the app crashes at this point, you probably added the privacy policy to one of the extension targets instead of the main app.

The Payload

When it's time to invite somebody to an event, you'll send a remote notification with a payload that looks like this:

```
{
  "aps": {
    "alert": {
        "title": "New Calendar Invitation"
    },
    "badge": 1,
    "mutable-content": 1,
    "category": "CalendarInvite"
  },
  "title": "Family Reunion",
  "start": "2022-08-20T08:00:00-08:00",
  "end": "2022-08-20T12:00:00-08:00",
  "id": 12
}
```

Notice that you're setting the `mutable-content` key to `1` so that your service extension runs, as well as a `category` so that your custom UI extension is triggered. The last four fields simply specify the details of the event.

This packet structure also assumes that your server is tracking the calendar invitations to know who accepted and rejected them, which is why there is an `id` key which uniquely identifies this invitation in your database. To make life easy, the dates use the **ISO8601** date format.

Notification Service Extension

The goal of your remote push notification is to provide a custom user interface to accept/reject/comment on the calendar invitation that's sent to the end user. What happens if the end user doesn't allow calendar access? It would be pretty strange to pop up the UI asking them to take action.

Even though you can't stop a notification from going through, you *can* change the notification. In this case, that means that you should check if calendar permissions are granted.

What action do you think you could take if permission is denied? The simplest solution is to remove the category from the payload, which would prevent the custom UI from appearing at all!

The pieces to be implemented in the service extension are threefold:

1. Remove the category if calendar permissions aren't granted.
2. Update the app icon badge.
3. Update the body of the notification.

Spend some time trying to implement those three items yourself and then come back to see the way the goals are accomplished, here.

Validating Calendar Permissions

Modify **NotificationService.swift**, in the **Payload Modification** target, to include an import of `EventKit`:

```
import EventKit
```

Then update `didReceive(_:withContentHandler:)` to blank out the `category` field of the payload if calendar permissions are denied by adding this check to the bottom of the method:

```
if EKEventStore.authorizationStatus(for: .event) != .authorized
{
  bestAttemptContent.categoryIdentifier = ""
}
```

Setting `categoryIdentifier` to an empty string will ensure the content UI doesn't display.

App Badging

It's time to add a badge to your app's icon for when a new notification comes in. The first step is to create an **App Group**. If you don't remember how to do this, follow the steps shown in Chapter 10, "Modifying the Payload".

Badging the app is handled by using the App Group you created and the `UserDefaults` class. Create a new Swift file called **UserDefaults.swift** in the **CoolCalendar** target with code to set an integer in the proper App Group. Be sure you update the name of the suite to match what you called the App Group!

```
import Foundation

extension UserDefaults {
  static let appGroup = UserDefaults(suiteName:
"group.com.yourcompany.CoolCalendar")!

  private enum Keys {
    static let badge = "badge"
  }

  var badge: Int {
    get {
      return integer(forKey: Keys.badge)
    } set {
      set(newValue, forKey: Keys.badge)
    }
  }
}
```

Since you're going to use this file in both the primary target and the service extension, click on the newly created file and, in the **File Inspector**, check **Payload Modification** inside **Target membership**.

With that done, you can now add a method to **NotificationService.swift** to update the badge:

```
private func updateBadge() {
  guard
    let bestAttemptContent,
    let increment = bestAttemptContent.badge as? Int
  else {
    return
  }

  if increment == 0 {
    UserDefaults.appGroup.badge = 0
    bestAttemptContent.badge = 0
  } else {
    let current = UserDefaults.appGroup.badge
    let new = current + increment

    UserDefaults.appGroup.badge = new
    bestAttemptContent.badge = NSNumber(value: new)
  }
}
```

When the service extension completes, iOS will set the badge on your app icon to the value specified in the payload. You've handled the update here by incrementing the *existing* badge count based on what was sent in the payload so that the count properly increments after each invitation is received.

When the user runs the app, you'll of course want to blank the badge count out. Edit **CoolCalendarApp.swift** and grab the scene phase from the environment by adding the following to the struct:

```
@Environment(\.scenePhase)
private var scenePhase
```

When the scene moves to an active state you'll want to blank out the badge count. Add the following method:

```
private func clearBadgeCount(phase: ScenePhase) {
  guard phase == .active else { return }

  UserDefaults.appGroup.badge = 0
  UIApplication.shared.applicationIconBadgeNumber = 0
}
```

If the phase isn't moving to an active state there's nothing to do. However, when the app becomes active, you'll clear out the badge.

You'll notice that the `UserDefaults` extension wasn't technically necessary here as you're not decrementing based on which invitations you've seen. In a normal production app, however, you'd only want to decrement the count when the user actually sees the specific invitations that were new.

All that's left to do is call that method. Add the following line to the body, just after putting the managed object context into the environment.

```
.onChange(of: scenePhase, perform: clearBadgeCount)
```

Notification Body

The final task is parsing your custom payload data and updating the body of the notification message to something more user friendly.

Add the following method inside the class in **NotificationService.swift**:

```
private func updateText(request: UNNotificationRequest) {
  guard let bestAttemptContent else { return }

  let formatter = ISO8601DateFormatter()
  let authStatus = EKEventStore.authorizationStatus(for: .event)

  guard authStatus == .authorized,
    let userInfo = request.content.userInfo as? [String: Any],
    let title = userInfo["title"] as? String,
```

```
      !title.isEmpty,
      let start = userInfo["start"] as? String,
      let startDate = formatter.date(from: start),
      let end = userInfo["end"] as? String,
      let endDate = formatter.date(from: end),
      userInfo["id"] as? Int != nil
    else {
      bestAttemptContent.categoryIdentifier = ""
      return
    }

    let rangeFormatter = DateIntervalFormatter()
    rangeFormatter.dateStyle = .short
    rangeFormatter.timeStyle = .short

    let range = rangeFormatter.string(from: startDate, to:
  endDate)
    bestAttemptContent.body = "\(title)\n\(range)"
  }
```

Notice how, if any piece of the required payload is missing, or in an incorrect format, the `categoryIdentifier` is blanked out. It doesn't make sense to let the custom UI code get called when it would simply fail. Two separate `guard` clauses are required, as Swift will not allow access to `bestAttemptContent` in the failure condition of a `guard` clause where that variable is checked.

Using ISO8601 dates is very convenient, as Apple has provided a parser explicitly for that format! As long as the payload contains all the expected keys in the proper date formats, the body is updated to include the title and the date range. With dates, you'll always want to utilize the provided classes, such as `DateIntervalFormatter` to ensure that the user's locale is properly respected.

While nothing needs to be done with the invitation ID, you still want to ensure that it exists in the payload so that you know there's valid content to pass to the Content Service Extension.

All that's left to do in this file is to call both of the methods that you just implemented from `didReceive` just before the completion handler is called. Your final `didReceive(_:withContentHandler)` method should now look like this:

```
  self.contentHandler = contentHandler
  bestAttemptContent = (request.content.mutableCopy() as?
  UNMutableNotificationContent)

  guard let bestAttemptContent else {
    return
  }
```

```
defer { contentHandler(bestAttemptContent) }

if EKEventStore.authorizationStatus(for: .event) != .authorized
{
  bestAttemptContent.categoryIdentifier = ""
}

updateBadge()
updateText(request: request)
```

Phew! There's almost more text explaining what to do than it actually takes to do it! You can see how modifying the payload might seem daunting at first, but you can take significant action with very little code. The net benefit to your end users is a much better experience, which always makes the little bit of extra effort worth it.

In a production app there are other considerations you might want to take into account, such as:

- What about all-day events?
- What about recurring events?
- What if the title is an empty string?
- What happens if you send a start date that comes after an end date?

This is a great time to build and run the app again and send yourself a push notification. As a reminder, here's a payload you can test with:

```
{
  "aps": {
    "alert": {
        "title": "New Calendar Invitation"
    },
    "badge": 1,
    "mutable-content": 1,
    "category": "CalendarInvite"
  },
  "title": "Family Reunion",
  "start": "2022-08-20T08:00:00-08:00",
  "end": "2022-08-20T12:00:00-08:00",
  "id": 12
}
```

You can do this with the **PushNotifications** tester app as described in Chapter 5, "Sending Your First Push Notification." You can find the payload at the start of this chapter.

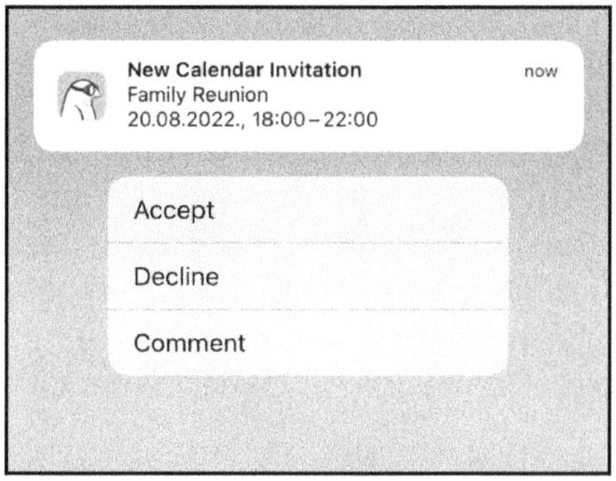

Has the body of the text message been updated properly? If there's no change, make sure you remembered to set `mutable-content` to `1` in the `aps` part of the payload. If it's still not working, refer back to Chapter 10, "Modifying the Payload", for help.

Those goodies in your kitchen aren't going to eat themselves. You've done some great work so grab yourself a snack, take a quick break and then it'll be time to work on the user interface.

Content Service Extension

Instead of just asking for a response, wouldn't it be nicer to show your users what their calendars look like for the time period related to the new event that they were invited to? To do this, you'll use a library called **CalendarKit** that the starter project has included. As the goal here isn't to teach you how to use CalendarKit, the starter project already includes the code related to that library for you.

Considering what the goals of the UI will be leads to the following five tasks:

1. Set the **Info.plist** details related to the category that you're using.
2. Add the newly arrived invitation to CalendarKit.
3. Display all events happening at the same time as the new event.
4. If the user accepts the invite, add it to iOS's calendar.
5. If the user comments, update the server.

It probably seems a bit silly to list out such simple tasks, but thinking of the UI tasks ahead of time helps to break down what, at first, seems like a daunting challenge into manageable pieces that you can focus on.

Updating the Info.plist

Open up **Info.plist** inside of the **Custom UI** target folder and expand out the **NSExtension** key *all the way*, as you learned to do in Chapter 11, "Custom Interfaces". Inside **NSExtensionAttributes**, you'll need to add the **UNNotificationExtensionCategory** key with a value to match what you set the `categoryIdentifier` to be in **AppDelegate.swift**. If you've used the same category name as the book example, that means you'll need to put **CalendarInvite** as the value.

Since the calendar itself will contain the details of the notification, it's definitely not desirable to have iOS display the body of the notification in the UI. I know, I know... right now you're thinking to yourself, "What?! Then why did I *just* edit the body of the notification to be human readable?" Remember that you might have had to disable the custom UI portion. If it gets disabled, you'd still want a nice text message. If it's not, then you want the visual UI.

Create a new `Boolean` key, under **NSExtensionAttributes**, named `UNNotificationExtensionDefaultContentHidden` and set the value to `YES`.

Adding Information to CalendarKit

You'll have to do the same extraction from the payload that you did in the Notification Service Extension, but, this time, there's no need to check for calendar access because, if you get here, it's guaranteed to be "on" as you just checked it in the Notification Service Extension.

In **NotificationViewController.swift**'s `didReceive(_:)`, after you do the parsing, you'll want to send the invitation details into CalendarKit. Add the below code just after the line that adds the timeline container as a subview:

```
let formatter = ISO8601DateFormatter()

guard
  let userInfo = notification.request.content.userInfo as?
[String: Any],
  let title = userInfo["title"] as? String, !title.isEmpty,
  let start = userInfo["start"] as? String,
  let startDate = formatter.date(from: start),
  let end = userInfo["end"] as? String,
```

```
    let endDate = formatter.date(from: end),
    let id = userInfo["id"] as? Int else {
    return
  }

  var appointments = [
    addCalendarKitEvent(start: startDate, end: endDate, title:
  title)
  ]
```

Getting Nearby Calendar Items

Now that the new invitation is squared away, you'll need to find the events in the users' existing calendars that will occur around the same date/time. It's probably a good idea to consider a couple of hours before and after the event so that your users can plan for drive times, doctors always being late to the start of an appointment or other buffers of time needed.

Start off by creating a property for the event store to the top of `NotificationViewController`:

```
private let eventStore = EKEventStore()
```

Add the following code to the bottom of `didRecieve(_:)`, before the commented out lines:

```
let calendar = Calendar.current
let displayStart = calendar.date(byAdding: .hour, value: -2, to:
startDate)!
let displayEnd = calendar.date(byAdding: .hour, value: 2, to:
endDate)!

let predicate = eventStore.predicateForEvents(
  withStart: displayStart,
  end: displayEnd,
  calendars: nil
)

appointments += eventStore
  .events(matching: predicate)
  .map {
    addCalendarKitEvent(
      start: $0.startDate,
      end: $0.endDate,
      title: $0.title,
      cgColor: $0.calendar.cgColor)
  }
```

In the above code, you first determine what time is two hours before the invitation and two hours after. You then search for all of the user's calendar events in that window of time using a predicate. Finally, you add all of those events to the calendar view using CalendarKit.

In a production app, you'd need to do some extra checks to see how long the appointment is, for example, or whether it's an all-day event; you'd then need to modify the times accordingly. Never just add seconds to a date thinking it's the right thing to do. Always use the built-in calendrical calculations that `Foundation` provides so that you don't get caught by leap years, leap seconds, missing midnight hours and a slew of other time-related issues.

After adding the above code, uncomment the commented-out lines related to the `timelineContainer`. Those lines are necessary to make CalendarKit work properly but, until `displayStart` and `displayEnd` were defined, they would have resulted in confusing compiler errors.

Build and run the app, and send yourself another push notification. When you long-press into the notification, you should see a UI showing the time slot for the new event, as well as any events you might have planned at the same time.

You can play with the time in the payload to test out different appointments.

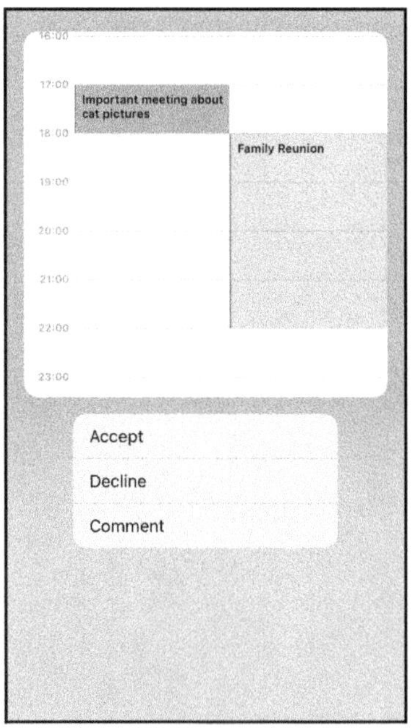

Accepting and Declining

The UI is now displaying a snapshot of part of the calendar so that the end user can make an informed decision about whether or not to accept the invitation. What happens when they accept or reject, though? You'll want to determine which option was chosen and then take some action, such as connecting to a REST endpoint to store the response.

If the invitation is declined, you'll probably want to update your server so it can process the event, and eventually you'll dismiss the UI. There's now an issue to consider: The `didReceive(_:completionHandler:)` method, which responds to the action buttons, has no idea what the event is. You'll fix that by adding another property to the class:

```
private var calendarIdentifier: Int?
```

Then set that in `didReceive(_:)` just after decoding the payload.

```
calendarIdentifier = id
```

You can now implement the `didReceive(_:completionHandler:)` method to start handling the actions by adding the following to the bottom of the `UNNotificationContentExtension` extension:

```
func didReceive(
    _ response: UNNotificationResponse
) async -> UNNotificationContentExtensionResponseOption {
  guard
    let choice = ActionIdentifier(rawValue:
response.actionIdentifier)
  else {
    // This shouldn't happen but definitely don't crash.
    // Let the users report a bug that nothing happens
    // for this choice so you can fix it.
    return .doNotDismiss
  }

  switch choice {
  case .accept, .decline:
    return .dismissAndForwardAction
  case .comment:
    return .doNotDismiss
  }
}
```

Are you getting a compiler error that `ActionIdentifier` is unknown? You know the drill! Add **Custom UI** to its target membership.

If the user chooses to enter a comment, bring up the keyboard and tell the completion handler that the UI window should stay active. If they accept or decline the invitation, the window can simply be dismissed.

You're using a new option here, called `dismissAndForward`, which tells the UI to dismiss, while also forwarding the notification onto your primary app, triggering the `userNotificationCenter(_:didReceive:)` method.

Because this app wants to display the responses to each invite in a table, it's necessary to store the response in a Core Data entity. While it's entirely possible to create a new entity in an extension target, it's *not* easy to know that it happened in the main target. Both targets would use the same root context from the `NSPersistentContainer`, and `Foundation`'s notifications don't cross app targets. For this reason, it's simpler to leave the Core Data work to the primary app target. You'll handle that in just a bit.

Commenting on the Invitation

This one takes a little more work to handle properly. You want to be able to comment without the notification being dismissed as soon as you do. In order to make that happen, you've got to tell iOS that you're willing to become the first responder (i.e., provide a custom keyboard) and handle input by overriding `canBecomeFirstResponder`.

Add the following override to the top of `NotificationViewController`:

```
override var canBecomeFirstResponder: Bool {
  return true
}
```

When a keyboard appears from iOS, there's no way for you to get access to the `UITextField` that is presented. Since you need to know when the **Return** button is pressed, it's therefore necessary to replace the `UITextField` Apple provides with one of your own. The starter project has already created the `keyboardInputAccessoryView` for you for just this purpose.

By embedding the text field inside of another view, you can give some shading to the outer view, making the text field easier to see. Remember that you're using full `UIKit`-based controls here, so you can add as many features as you need such as buttons and date pickers to suggest new times. Just always keep the user experience in mind as you add more controls.

The delegate has to be set on the `keyboardTextField` so that you can catch when the user taps the **Return** button on the keyboard to dismiss it.

Add the following to the top of `textFieldShouldReturn(_:)`:

```
guard
  textField == keyboardTextField,
  let text = textField.text,
  let calendarIdentifier = calendarIdentifier
else {
  return true
}

Server.shared.commentOnInvitation(with: calendarIdentifier,
comment: text)
textField.text = nil

keyboardTextField.resignFirstResponder()
resignFirstResponder()
```

Something that's not immediately obvious until after you've done some UI testing is that the comment text the end user typed won't automatically disappear as the same `UITextField` is utilized each time the keyboard appears.

That's why it's necessary to set the text field's `text` property to `nil` to properly clear it when you're done.

Of course, for iOS to know that you want to actually do something with the `UIView` that you just created, you've got to tell it so!

Add this override to the top of the class:

```
override var inputAccessoryView: UIView? {
  return keyboardInputAccessoryView
}
```

All that's left to do is to display the keyboard when the **Comment** button is tapped inside the `switch` in the async version of `didReceive(_:)`:

```
case .comment:
  _ = becomeFirstResponder()
  _ = keyboardTextField.becomeFirstResponder()
  return .doNotDismiss
```

Build and run.

Send yourself some events and you should see your snazzy new custom UI with usable buttons!

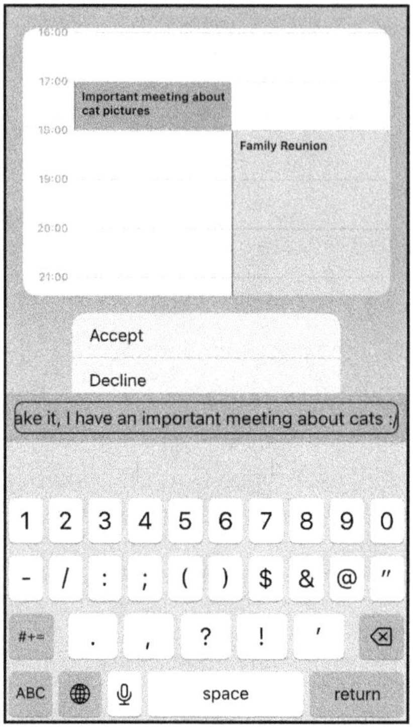

Show Your Responses

After sending some notifications, it'll quickly become apparent that nothing is happening in the main app when you accept or reject a notification. You never actually create and display a Core Data entity anywhere. Time to resolve that issue!

Create Core Data Entities

Head over to **NotificationCenter.swift** one last time. As mentioned, you'll generate the Core Data entities from one of `UNUserNotificationCenterDelegate`'s methods. Add an import so you can use Core Data:

```
import CoreData
```

If the user accepts or declines the invitation, you'll need to store that response in your Core Data model. Add the following method to the class:

```
private func createInvite(
  with title: String,
  starting: Date,
  ending: Date,
  accepted: Bool
) async {
  let context =
PersistenceController.shared.container.viewContext
  await context.perform(schedule: .enqueued) {
    let invite = Invite(context: context)
    invite.title = title
    invite.start = starting
    invite.end = ending
    invite.accepted = accepted

    try? context.save()
  }
}
```

For this example app you'll just ignore any save errors, which is why you used `try?`. In a real app you'd likely want to take some action if the save were to fail.

Now you'll need to take appropriate action based on the user's response to the invitation. Add the following method to the `UNUserNotificationCenterDelegate` extension:

```
@MainActor
func userNotificationCenter(
  _ center: UNUserNotificationCenter,
  didReceive response: UNNotificationResponse
) async {
  let formatter = ISO8601DateFormatter()
  let content = response.notification.request.content

  guard
    let choice = ActionIdentifier(rawValue:
response.actionIdentifier),
    let userInfo = content.userInfo as? [String: Any],
    let title = userInfo["title"] as? String, !title.isEmpty,
    let start = userInfo["start"] as? String,
    let startDate = formatter.date(from: start),
    let end = userInfo["end"] as? String,
    let endDate = formatter.date(from: end),
    let calendarIdentifier = userInfo["id"] as? Int
  else {
      return
  }
}
```

The parsing is no different than before, but notice that there are a couple extra "dot walks" that have to happen to get to the `userInfo` property. Even though you know for a fact that everything will parse properly, it's never a good idea to use force unwrapping if there's another way; the `guard` syntax is a better choice here.

All that's left to do is to update the server with the user's decision and create a Core Data entity, which will then automatically be displayed in the table on the main view.

To do this, add the following code to the bottom of the above method:

```
switch choice {
case .accept:
  Server.shared.acceptInvitation(with: calendarIdentifier)
  await createInvite(with: title, starting: startDate, ending:
endDate, accepted: true)
case .decline:
  Server.shared.declineInvitation(with: calendarIdentifier)
  await createInvite(with: title, starting: startDate, ending:
endDate, accepted: false)
default:
  break
}
```

Define the Detail Cell View

To prove that everything is working correctly you'll want to display the invite's details. You'll be generating a list row that looks like so:

There are three distinct piece to the row:

1. The thumbs up or thumbs down image depending on whether or not the invitation was accepted.
2. The name of the invitation.
3. The date range of the invitation.

Create a new SwiftUI View file in your main target called **AcceptanceImage.swift**, so that you can display the proper thumb image:

```
import SwiftUI

struct AcceptanceImage: View {
  let accepted: Bool

  var body: some View {
    if accepted {
      Image(systemName: "hand.thumbsup")
        .foregroundColor(.green)
    } else {
      Image(systemName: "hand.thumbsdown")
        .foregroundColor(.red)
    }
  }
}

struct AcceptanceImage_Previews: PreviewProvider {
  static var previews: some View {
    Group {
      AcceptanceImage(accepted: true)
        .previewLayout(.fixed(width: 50, height: 50))
      AcceptanceImage(accepted: false)
        .previewLayout(.fixed(width: 50, height: 50))
    }
  }
}
```

Remember that in SwiftUI `View` objects are cheap, and Apple recommends breaking your views into smaller chunks. The preceding code will take a `Bool` to the constructor and then either display a green thumbs up or a red thumbs down.

Apple has provided over 4,000 configurable images which are all available for your app to use. You can see all of the available symbols by looking at developer.apple.com/sf-symbols.

Now that you are able to display the proper thumb, it's time to create the rest of the cell. Create a new SwiftUI View file in your main target called **InviteRow.swift**.

You'll be working with your Core Data entities so add the appropriate import to the top of the file:

```
import CoreData
```

Since the intent of the row is to display the invitation details, add a variable to hold the invitation at the top of the `struct`:

```
let invite: Invite
```

Xcode is now unhappy that the preview isn't passing the required initializer parameter, so create a fake invitation by replacing the entire preview with the following code:

```
static var previews: some View {
  // 1
  let invite = Invite(context:
PersistenceController.preview.container.viewContext)

  // 2
  invite.title = "Event Name"
  invite.accepted = true
  invite.start = Date()
  invite.end = Date().addingTimeInterval(3600)

  // 3
  return InviteRow(invite: invite)
    .previewLayout(.fixed(width: 300, height: 100))
}
```

The code performs the following actions:

1. You are creating a new Core Data object in the *preview* container, not the *shared* container. The preview container uses the in-memory store for the simulator.
2. Generate any random data. While adding 3,600 seconds to a date in order to add an hour is always wrong in production code, it's perfectly fine for a preview.
3. Call the initializer with the newly generated Core Data object.

Now it's time to format the cell. Replace the default `Text` element in the body:

```
// 1
VStack(alignment: .leading) {
  // 2
  HStack {
    AcceptanceImage(accepted: invite.accepted)
    // 3
    Text(invite.title!)
      .font(.headline)
  }
}
```

1. Use a `VStack` since you want two lines in the cell. If you don't specify a `.leading` alignment the lines will be centered, which wouldn't look correct.
2. Your thumb image and the title should be side by side, thus the `HStack`.
3. Core data properties are always optionals, regardless of what you specified in the data model. Because you made the model attribute non-optional it's safe to force unwrap the title.

To display the date range you'll make use of a formatter. Define a formatter at the top of the file, just below the `import` statements:

```
private let dateFormatter: DateIntervalFormatter = {
  let formatter = DateIntervalFormatter()
  formatter.dateStyle = .short
  formatter.timeStyle = .short
  return formatter
}()
```

Never display dates directly, always use a formatter. Because you're showing a range of time `DateIntervalFormatter` is the proper class to use. Remember that Apple has specified SwiftUI `View` objects are cheap to create. That means they may be destroyed and created multiple times. It's therefore important that you place the formatter outside of the struct so that you aren't constantly recreating the formatter.

Now that you can show a date range properly, add the date just after the `HStack`:

```
Text(dateFormatter.string(from: invite.start!, to: invite.end!))
  .font(.subheadline)
```

Update ContentView

Edit **ContentView.swift** and add the Core Data code which will query all your invitations:

```
@FetchRequest(
  sortDescriptors: [NSSortDescriptor(keyPath: \Invite.start,
ascending: true)],
  animation: .default
)
private var invites: FetchedResults<Invite>
```

Then replace the default `Text` with a list displaying invitations, using the row you just created:

```
List(invites) { InviteRow(invite: $0) }
```

Build and run the app. Send yourself a few invites. When you open the app, you should see a list of accepted and declined appointments.

Where to Go From Here?

`@State` and bindings might be new concepts if you're not familiar with SwiftUI. You can take a look at episode 14 in our video tutorial, *Your First iOS & SwiftUI App: An App from Scratch*, available at bit.ly/3AYqomC.

If you need to brush up on your Core Data skills, take a look at *Core Data by Tutorials*, available at bit.ly/3oXTv1e.

And, with that, your project is finished! Even so, there is still one final category of notifications to cover: local notifications, which you will explore in the next chapter.

Chapter 13: Local Notifications

Although you've put together the key concepts up to this point, there is one more category of notifications to cover: local notifications.

While the vast majority of notifications displayed on your device are remote notifications, it's also possible to display notifications originating from the user's device, locally. There are three distinct types of local notifications:

1. **Calendar**: Notification occurs on a specific date.
2. **Interval**: Notification occurs after a specific amount of time.
3. **Location**: Notification occurs when entering a specific area.

While less frequently used, local notifications still play an important role for many apps. You should also challenge the immediate notion of using a remote notification. For example, if you provide a food-ordering app, it might want to tell the user that the food is ready to pick up. Will the restaurant really take action when the food is ready or could you, instead, use an interval-based local notification to send the alert after a 10-minute waiting period?

You Still Need Permission!

Even though the notification is created and delivered locally on the user's device, you must still obtain permission to display local notifications. Just like remote notifications, the user can grant or remove permissions at any time.

The only difference when requesting permissions locally is that you do *not* call the `registerForRemoteNotifications` method on success:

```
func registerForLocalNotifications(application: UIApplication) {
  let center = UNUserNotificationCenter.current()
  center.requestAuthorization(
    options: [.badge, .sound, .alert]) { granted, _ in
    guard granted else { return }
    // Take action here
  }
}
```

> **Note**: Since the user may revoke permissions at any time, view controllers creating a local notification must check for permission in `viewDidAppear`. If you're using SwiftUI, check for permissions inside the `onAppear(perform:)` method on your root view.

Objects Versus Payloads

The primary difference between remote and local notifications is how they are triggered. You've seen that remote notifications require some type of external service to send a JSON payload through APNs. Local notifications use all the same type of data that you provide in a JSON payload but they instead use Swift objects to define what is delivered to the user.

Creating a Trigger

Local notifications utilize what is referred to as a **trigger**, which is the condition under which the notification will be delivered to the user. There are three possible triggers, each corresponding to one of the notification types:

1. `UNCalendarNotificationTrigger`
2. `UNTimeIntervalNotificationTrigger`
3. `UNLocationNotificationTrigger`

All three triggers contain a `repeats` property, which allows you to fire the trigger more than once.

UNCalendarNotificationTrigger

Not surprisingly, this trigger occurs at specific points in time. While you might assume that you'd be using a `Date` to specify when the trigger goes off, you'll actually use `DateComponents`. A `Date` distinctly specifies one specific point in time, which isn't always helpful for a trigger. If you're using a calendar trigger, it's more likely that you only have *parts* of a date.

For example, you might want to trigger at 8:30 in the morning, or just on a Monday. Using `DateComponents` lets you specify as much of the requirements as necessary without being too explicit about the rest.

To have an alarm go off every Monday at 8:30 a.m., you'd write code like this:

```
let components = DateComponents(hour: 8, minute: 30, weekday: 2)
let trigger = UNCalendarNotificationTrigger(
  dateMatching: components,
  repeats: true)
```

UNTimeIntervalNotificationTrigger

This trigger is perfect for timers. You might want to display a notification after 10 minutes, rather than at a specific time. You just tell iOS how many seconds in the future the notification should be delivered. If you need the trigger to happen at a *specific* time, like 2 p.m., you should be using the `UNCalendarNotificationTrigger` instead to avoid numerous time zone issues related to dates.

In this example, after ordering food from an online service, you'll want to let the end user know to head out in 10 minutes to pick it up:

```
let trigger = UNTimeIntervalNotificationTrigger(
  timeInterval: 10 * 60,
  repeats: false)
```

UNLocationNotificationTrigger

If you're a fan of geocaching, this one's for you! Utilizing this trigger allows you to specify a `CLCircularRegion` that you wish to monitor. When the device enters said area, the notification will fire. You need to know the latitude and longitude of the center of your target location as well as the radius that should be used. Those three items define a circular region on the map, which iOS will monitor for entry.

> **Note**: You must have authorization to use **Core Location** and must have permission to monitor the user's location while they're using the app. You do not need to request to always have permission as just regions are being monitored.

You'll also need to let iOS know whether you care if the user is entering the region, exiting or both.

Please see "Core Location Tutorial for iOS: Tracking Visited Locations" (bit.ly/2MLc1GG) for more information on Core Location, privacy concerns and requesting permissions if you're not already familiar with that framework.

If, for example, you'd like to schedule a notification whenever the user enters a 1 mile radius around 1 Infinite Loop, Cupertino, California, you'd use code similar to the following:

```
let oneMile = Measurement(value: 1, unit: UnitLength.miles)
let radius = oneMile.converted(to: .meters).value
let coordinate = CLLocationCoordinate2D(
  latitude: 37.33182,
  longitude: -122.03118)
let region = CLCircularRegion(
  center: coordinate,
  radius: radius,
  identifier: UUID().uuidString)

region.notifyOnExit = false
region.notifyOnEntry = true
```

```
let trigger = UNLocationNotificationTrigger(
  region: region,
  repeats: false)
```

Defining Content

Excellent; you now know *when* the trigger is going to go off. It's time to tell iOS *what* should be presented in the notification. This is where the `UNMutableNotificationContent` class comes into play. Be sure to note the "`Mutable`" in that class's name. There's also a class called `UNNotificationContent`, which you won't use here or you'll end up with compiler errors.

You can think of this class as the equivalent of the JSON payload used in remote notifications. The elements from the `aps` dictionary exist as properties right on the object. For your custom content, you simply add that to the `userInfo` dictionary.

If you worked through Chapter 12, "Putting It All Together," then you'll remember working with a payload like so:

```
{
  "aps" : {
    "alert" : {
        "title" : "New Calendar Invitation"
    },
    "badge" : 1,
    "mutable-content" : 1,
    "category" : "CalendarInvite"
  },
  "title" : "Family Reunion",
  "start" : "2018-04-10T08:00:00-08:00",
  "end" : "2018-04-10T12:00:00-08:00",
  "id" : 12
}
```

You'd exactly mimic that same data with a local notification using the following code:

```
let content = UNMutableNotificationContent()
content.title = "New Calendar Invitation"
content.badge = 1
content.categoryIdentifier = "CalendarInvite"
content.userInfo = [
  "title": "Family Reunion",
  "start": "2018-04-10T08:00:00-08:00",
  "end": "2018-04-10T12:00:00-08:00",
  "id": 12
]
```

Notice how everything outside of your aps dictionary, meaning - your custom content, falls under the `userInfo` dictionary.

Playing Sounds

If you'd like your notification to play a sound when it's delivered, you must either store the file in your app's main bundle, or you must download it and store it in the **Library/Sounds** subdirectory of your app's container directory. Generally, you'll just want to use the default sound:

```
content.sound = UNNotificationSound.default
```

Please refer back to Chapter 3, "Remote Notification Payload," for full details on the requirements around playing sounds and which formats are supported.

Adding Localization

There's one small "gotcha" when working with localization and local notifications. Consider the case wherein the user's device is set to English, and you set the content to a localized value. Then, you create a trigger to fire in three hours. An hour from then, the user switches their device back to Arabic. Suddenly, you're showing the wrong language!

The solution to the above problem is to not use the normal `NSLocalizedString` methods. Instead, you should use `localizedUserNotificationString(forKey:arguments:)` from `NSString`. The difference is that the latter method delays loading the localized string until the notification is actually delivered, thus ensuring the localization is correct.

> **Note**: Always use `localizedUserNotificationString(forKey:arguments:)` when localizing local notifications.

Grouping Notifications

If you'd like your local notification to support grouping, simply set the `threadIdentifier` property with a proper identifier to group them by.

```
content.threadIdentifier = "My group identifier here"
```

Scheduling

Now that you've defined *when* the notification should occur and *what* to display, you simply need to ask iOS to take care of it for you:

```
let identifier = UUID().uuidString
let request = UNNotificationRequest(
  identifier: identifier,
  content: content,
  trigger: trigger)

UNUserNotificationCenter.current().add(request) { error in
  if let error {
    // Handle unfortunate error if one occurs.
  }
}
```

Each request needs to have a *unique* identifier so that you can refer to it later on if you wish to cancel the notification before it's actually fired. A UUID is unique by definition, so it's a great choice to use.

Foreground Notifications

Just like with remote notifications, you'll need to take an extra step to allow local notifications to be displayed when the app is running in the foreground. It's the exact same code that remote notifications use.

Simply adopt `UNUserNotificationCenterDelegate` somewhere in your app and implement the following method:

```
func userNotificationCenter(
  _ center: UNUserNotificationCenter,
  willPresent notification: UNNotification)
  async -> UNNotificationPresentationOptions
{
  return [.badge, .sound, .banner]
}
```

You can, of course, take other actions here such as updating the user interface directly based on what the notification is for!

The Sample Platter

That seems like quite enough reference material. Time to write some code! Please open up the starter project and set your team ID as discussed in Chapter 7, "Expanding the Application."

You'll notice that there's an awful lot of code in the starter project, but don't let that scare you. The intent of this chapter is for you to learn about local notifications, not have you spend a ton of time building a SwiftUI app to handle all three types of local notifications.

The general goal for this app is to allow the user to pick one of the three types of notifications, configure it and then see on the main view whether or not it's been delivered. The user will also be able to cancel any notifications that are still pending to be delivered.

Requesting Permission

Just like with remote notifications, the first task you'll need to take care of is getting your user's permission to send them local notifications.

Open **LocalNotifications.swift**. This file will manage everything related to local notifications. Start by adding the method which will request permissions:

```
func requestAuthorization() async throws {
  authorized = try await center.requestAuthorization(options:
[.badge, .sound, .alert])
}
```

The code is essentially the same as you've done throughout the book. The only difference is that you're just directly updating the authorized property, which will then be published to any other objects which are monitoring the value.

Determine Pending and Delivered Notifications

The stated goal of the app was to display both delivered and pending notifications. To identify all notifications which are pending, you'll use the `pendingNotificationRequests` method.

Create a new property in `LocalNotifications` to hold the list of pending notifications:

```
@Published var pending: [UNNotificationRequest] = []
```

Then populate that property by adding the following:

```
@MainActor
func refreshNotifications() async {
  pending = await center.pendingNotificationRequests()
}
```

You ask the notification center to provide a list of requests which have been scheduled, but not yet delivered. By assigning the results to the `pending` property, iOS will publish a notification to anything which is watching for changes.

Retrieving the list of already delivered notifications is essentially the same code, just a different property and method. Add a property to hold the notifications:

```
@Published var delivered: [UNNotification] = []
```

Next, add the following code to the end of `refreshNotifications`:

```
delivered = await center.deliveredNotifications()
```

While the code for both pending and delivered notifications looks almost exactly the same, take note of the fact that pending notifications are of type `UNNotificationRequest`, whereas delivered notifications are `UNNotification`. The `UNNotification` has a `request` property that lets you get at the `UNNotificationRequest` details.

> **Note**: Once a user deletes a notification from the Notification Center on their device, it will no longer appear in the list of delivered notifications.

Removing Notifications

Most well written apps, which display a list of items, will also provide a way to delete items. The user might have made a mistake in scheduling the notification, for example. Add the following methods to **LocalNotifications.swift**:

```
func removePendingNotifications(identifiers: [String]) async {
  center.removePendingNotificationRequests(withIdentifiers:
```

```
identifiers)
  await refreshNotifications()
}

func removeDeliveredNotifications(identifiers: [String]) async {
  center.removeDeliveredNotifications(withIdentifiers:
identifiers)
  await refreshNotifications()
}
```

`UNUserNotificationCenter` provides two separate methods to remove a notification. You must explicitly specify whether you're removing a pending or delivered notification as identifiers are not necessarily unique between the two types.

Be sure to refresh the notifications after removing items so that the pending and delivered lists are updated properly.

Configuring the Main View

It's time to make use of the class you just created. Open up **ContentView.swift** and add the following line to the top of the class:

```
@StateObject private var localNotifications =
LocalNotifications()
```

Marking *localNotifications* with the `@StateObject` property wrapper lets SwiftUI know that the containing class owns management of the property.

Next, find the line that configures the sheet. When the sheet is dismissed, you'll want to refresh the notifications.

```
.sheet(isPresented: $showSheet) {
  Task { await localNotifications.refreshNotifications() }
```

To display notifications in the `View`, your users have to have granted permissions. Request the permissions when the view appears by adding the following code to the end of `body`:

```
.task { try? await localNotifications.requestAuthorization() }
```

Now, when the view appears, the app will check for authorization. If authorization isn't granted you won't be able to display anything.

Next, add the following block of code inside the `Group` at the top of the body:

```
if !localNotifications.authorized {
  Text("This app only works when notifications are enabled.")
} else {
}
```

Hopefully that `Text` is never displayed for long! When permissions are granted, you'll want to display a list of pending notifications. Add a `List` inside of the `else` block:

```
List {
  // 1
  Section(header: Text("Pending")) {
    // 2
    ForEach(localNotifications.pending, id: \.identifier) {
      // 3
      HistoryCell(for: $0)
    }
  }
}
// 4
.listStyle(GroupedListStyle())
```

The preceding code accomplishes the following:

1. You're creating a `Section` inside of the `List` with a title of Pending to show the notifications which are scheduled, but not yet delivered.
2. You're iterating over each pending notification. The `ForEach` call requires that the data being iterated over conforms to `Identifiable`. If it doesn't, then you have to explicitly tell it the unique identifier. Since `UNNotificationRequest` provides a unique identifier, you can simply use that.
3. The notification is displayed via the supplied `HistoryCell` view.
4. You style the `List` makes to look like a grouped list.

Now add another `Section`, just below the first, to display the delivered notifications.

```
Section(header: Text("Delivered")) {
  ForEach(localNotifications.delivered, id:
\.request.identifier) {
    HistoryCell(for: $0.request)
  }
}
```

Notice that this time, the ID provided is slightly different. A `UNNotification` doesn't have an identifier. However, it does have a reference to the request which was sent. Thus, you can use that for the identifier.

Now that you can display the row, let's add a way to remove them. Just after the first `ForEach`, tell SwiftUI which method to call when a row is deleted by adding this line:

```
.onDelete(perform: deletePendingNotification)
```

Then, add the appropriate method to your `struct`:

```
private func deletePendingNotification(at offsets: IndexSet) {
  let identifiers = offsets.map {
    localNotifications.pending[$0].identifier
  }

  Task {
    await
localNotifications.removePendingNotifications(identifiers:
identifiers)
  }
}
```

When deleting a row, SwiftUI provides you with a list of integers via an `IndexSet`. That set represents each row which has been deleted. Using `map`, you transform the index of the row, which is also the index of the pending array, into the notifications identifier. Once you have the list of identifiers which should be removed you can pass them to the class you wrote to handle notifications.

Just like when configuring the sheet, you need to handle the fact that the delete to swipe action is not `async`-aware.

At first glance it seems odd to receive an `IndexSet`. If you swipe a row, that's a single value. It's nice to provide your users a way to delete multiple rows, though.

Find the line in the body which looks like this:

```
.navigationBarItems(trailing: Button {
```

And replace it with this:

```
.navigationBarItems(leading: EditButton(), trailing: Button {
```

That simple change now gives your view a way to edit multiple items at once. Build and run the app.

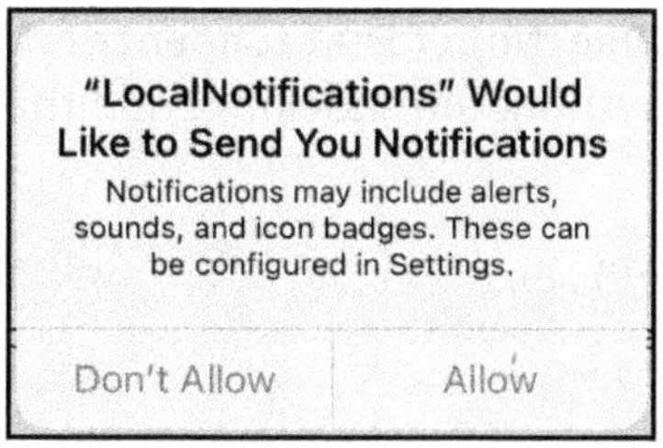

As expected, you're asked right away to grant permissions. Say yes...you know you want to. You should see your two `List` sections as well as an Edit button.

Scheduling Notifications

While there are more options available on the content of a notification, for the sample app, you'll only be using the `title`, `sound` and `badge` properties of the `UNMutableNotificationContent`.

Creating Content

Edit the **LocalNotifications.swift** file to add the following code to the bottom of the class:

```
func scheduleNotification(trigger: UNNotificationTrigger, model:
CommonFieldsModel) async throws {
  let title =
model.title.trimmingCharacters(in: .whitespacesAndNewlines)

  let content = UNMutableNotificationContent()
  content.title = title.isEmpty ? "No Title Provided" : title

  if model.hasSound {
    content.sound = UNNotificationSound.default
  }

  if let number = Int(model.badge) {
    content.badge = NSNumber(value: number)
  }
}
```

Pretty straightforward, right? You set the content object as described earlier in this chapter.

Adding the Request

Now that the content and trigger are in place, all that's left to do is create the request and hand it off to `UNUserNotificationCenter`. You've already seen the code for this, so it shouldn't be anything too shocking. Add the following to the end of the method:

```
let identifier = UUID().uuidString
let request = UNNotificationRequest(
  identifier: identifier,
  content: content,
  trigger: trigger)

try await center.add(request)
```

While the request has to have a unique identifier, you don't really have a need to know what it is, so using a `UUID` is a great choice here. If the request wasn't successfully added to the list of pending local notifications, then you'll tell the caller about the issue via the closure.

Head back over to **ContentView.swift** and call the method you just wrote from `scheduleNotification(trigger:model:)`

```
Task {
  do {
    try await localNotifications.scheduleNotification(trigger:
trigger, model: commonFields)
  } catch {
    alertText = AlertText(text: error.localizedDescription)
  }
}
```

If the notification failed to schedule, iOS will throw an exception with the failure. You then create an `AlertText` from that message.

Time Interval Notifications

You're almost ready to run the app and see something! The first notification trigger to implement is the `UNTimeIntervalNotificationTrigger`. With the methods you just created, you'll only need two lines of code now to set up a time-interval trigger. Open **TimeIntervalView.swift** and take a look at `doneButtonTapped`. Once the number of seconds to wait is known, you need to create the trigger just like you learned about earlier in the chapter.

Add this code to the end of the method, right before dismissing the modal:

```
let trigger = UNTimeIntervalNotificationTrigger(
  timeInterval: interval,
  repeats: model.isRepeating)

try await onComplete(trigger, model)
```

Calling the completion handler causes the `scheduleNotification(trigger:model:)` method in **ContentView.swift** to be called.

It's finally time to try things out! Build and run the app. You should have no errors at this point. There's a single warning which you'll fix up in a bit.

Tap the + button in the navigation bar and choose to add a timed trigger.

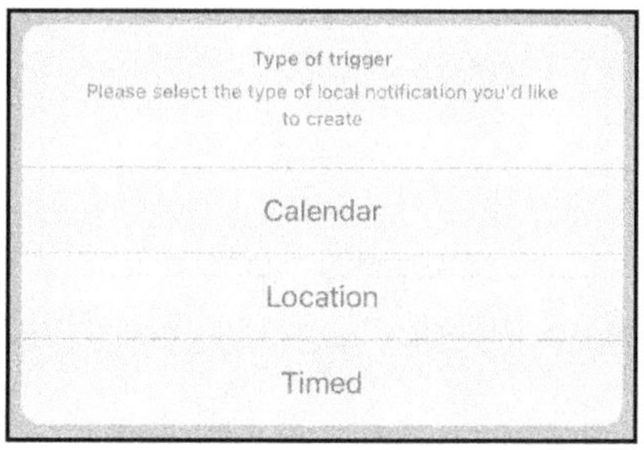

You'll be presented with a simple screen where you can specify how many seconds in the future the notification should trigger. While you must specify a title, the badge is optional. If you include a numeric value, then the app icon will be badged appropriately. If you specify a 10-second wait period and tap the **Done** button, you'll be returned to the home screen with a view like the following:

Wait for 10 seconds and the notification should appear. What? It didn't appear? Why not?

Just like when handling remote push notifications, local notifications will not appear when the app is running unless you tell it to.

Head back over to **LocalNotifications** and add this extension to the bottom of the file.

```
extension LocalNotifications: UNUserNotificationCenterDelegate {
  func userNotificationCenter(
    _ center: UNUserNotificationCenter,
    willPresent notification: UNNotification
  ) async -> UNNotificationPresentationOptions {
```

```
    return [.banner, .badge, .sound]
  }
}
```

The code is no different than what you have done for remote notifications. All that's left to do is assign the delegate. Add an initializer to `LocalNotifications`:

```
override init() {
  super.init()
  center.delegate = self
}
```

Build and run again. This time, after waiting the appropriate amount of time, you should see the notification appear.

Location Notifications

Handling locations takes just a bit more work.

Requesting Location Permissions

To enable the location to trigger a notification, you need to know the user's location. This means you first need to ask the user's permission to access their location.

Open the **Info.plist** file and add the privacy key for access to the user's location. The key's name is "**Privacy - Location When In Use Usage Description**".

Set its value to the string: "To know when you arrive at the target region."

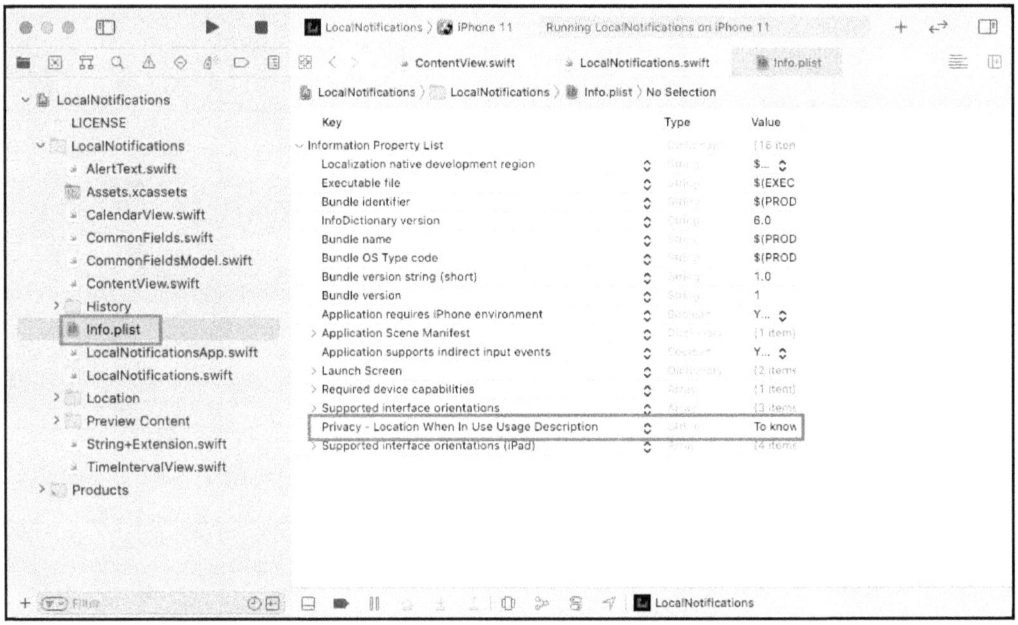

The **LocationManager.swift** file contains the boilerplate code necessary for requesting location authorization. You just need to make use of it.

Edit **LocationLookupView.swift** and grab a copy of the location manager from the environment:

```
@EnvironmentObject private var locationManager: LocationManager
```

The starter project put that object into the environment for you via the **LocalNotificationsApp.swift** file.

You shouldn't display the location form if the user isn't allowing location tracking, so replace the `body` in **LocationLookupView.swift** to wrap its contents in an `if` check:

```
if locationManager.authorized {
  LocationForm(onComplete: onComplete)
} else {
  Text(locationManager.authorizationErrorMessage)
}
```

If the user has authorized location tracking then you'll display the location form. If they have not, then you'll display the appropriate error message.

You'll want to ask for permissions as soon as this view appears, which means adding the normal SwiftUI `onAppear` call. You can't directly place that on an `if` block though, so wrap it in a `Group` instead.

```
Group {
  if locationManager.authorized {
    LocationForm(onComplete: onComplete)
  } else {
    Text(locationManager.authorizationErrorMessage)
  }
}
.onAppear(perform: locationManager.requestAuthorization)
```

Build and run your app. This time, after tapping the + button, choose Location. You should be presented with a request to allow your app to determine the user's location.

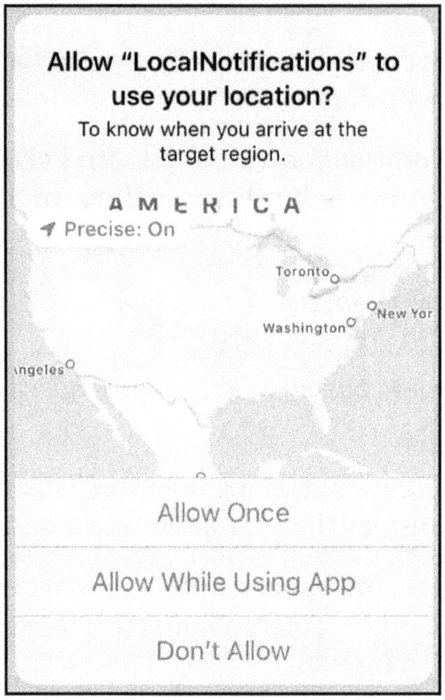

Now, you can start working on the actual trigger. In **LocationForm.swift**, you'll again edit the `doneButtonTapped` action to create the trigger. Add the following code to the method just before the last line which dismisses the modal and inside the `Task` block:

```
guard let coordinates = model.coordinate else {
  return
}

let region = CLCircularRegion(
  center: coordinates,
  radius: distance,
  identifier: UUID().uuidString)

region.notifyOnExit = model.notifyOnExit
region.notifyOnEntry = model.notifyOnEntry

let trigger = UNLocationNotificationTrigger(region: region,
repeats: commonFields.isRepeating)
try await onComplete(trigger, commonFields)
```

Similar to a timed notification, you're pulling values from the model and then creating the trigger. Scheduling is handled by your callback, just like before.

Build and run, again choosing a Location notification. The first screen you see allows you to specify an address and see a view of it on the map. Enter any address you like and tap the **Search** button. If you gave a valid address, you should see your destination.

I don't know about you, but I'm headed to the Louvre in Paris!

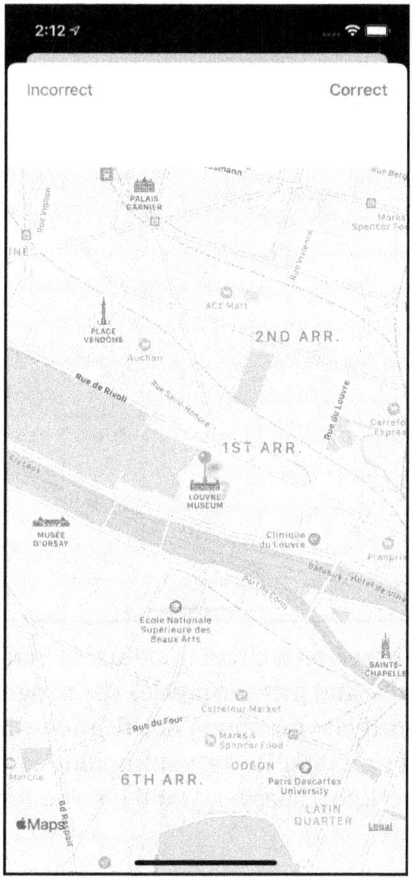

After you've entered a valid address, tap on the **Correct** button in the navigation bar.

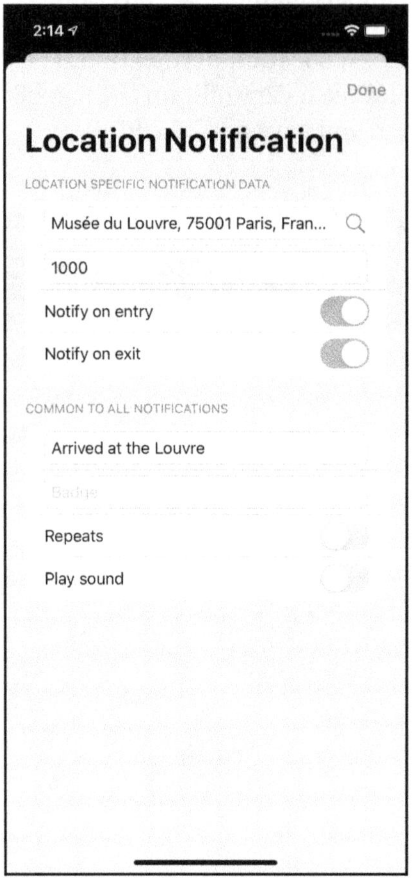

Location notifications are based on a circular radius, so you'll have to specify how many *meters* you'd like to use and provide a title. The badge is again optional but, this time, you can also identify if you want a notification when you enter the area, leave the area or both. After tapping **Done**, you should see your trigger in the Pending section. To complete this chapter, you'll have to book a flight to Paris and head over to the Louvre.

Calendar Notifications

Just one notification to go! Calendar-based local notifications, as discussed earlier, use the `DateComponents` `struct` to specify exactly when the notification will trigger. If you've worked with `DateComponents` before, you know how many different properties are available to you. For the sample app, to keep things simple, you're just using hours, minutes and seconds.

In **CalendarView.swift**, you'll see that `doneButtonTapped` has pulled out the details of the time for you already. All you've got to do is create the trigger to fire at the right time. Add the following code at the end of the method, just before dismissing the alert:

```
let trigger = UNCalendarNotificationTrigger(
  dateMatching: components,
  repeats: commonFields.isRepeating)

try await onComplete(trigger, commonFields)
```

Build and run your app one final time, and you'll be able to schedule a calendar-based local notification.

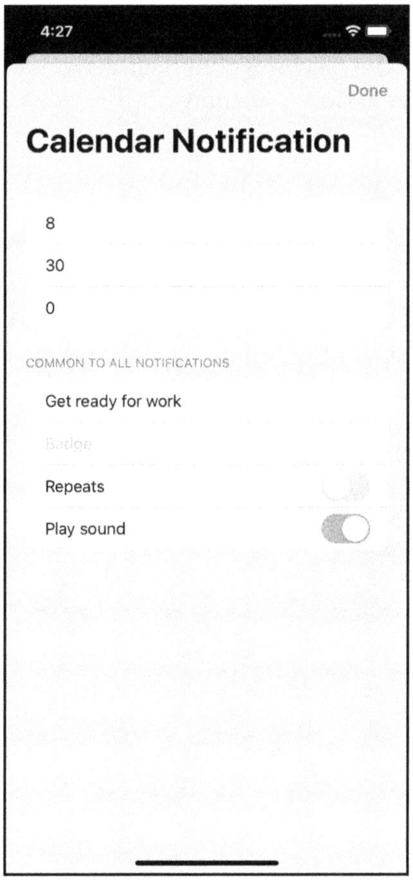

You've managed to utilize all the local notification types in a sample app. Hopefully, you've seen how easy the notification-related code is to implement.

Key Points

- While most push notifications displayed on your device are remote notifications, it's also possible to display notifications originating from the user's device, locally.
- Local notifications are less frequently used but they still merit your understanding. There may be times when a user needs a notification (like a reminder) free of any action being taken.
- **Calendar** notifications occur on a specific date or time.
- **Interval** notifications occur *after* a specific amount of time.
- **Location** notifications occur when entering a specific area.
- Even though the notification is created and delivered locally on the user's device, you must still obtain permission to display notifications.

Where to Go From Here?

In your own apps, you'll likely want to explore other concepts such as custom sounds, more options around calendar selection, and even custom actions and user interfaces. Refer back to each of the following chapters for information on how to add each feature to your local notifications:

- Chapter 9, "Custom Actions."
- Chapter 10, "Modifying the Payload."
- Chapter 11, "Custom Interfaces."

Chapter 14: watchOS

Local and remote notifications are a great way to inform your users about new or relevant information. There may be new content available, it might be their turn in the game or they may have just won the lottery. If your app has an accompanying iPhone app that supports notifications, by default, your Apple Watch will display the notification when appropriate. However, you can do better!

Where Did It Go?

Apple tries to determine the best target device to receive a notification. If you only have an Apple Watch, it'll go there. However, if you use a watch and another device, the destination depends not only on the type of notification but also on its source.

The diagram below will help you understand how Apple chooses which device should display the notification. As you can see, the notification type, whether it is Local, Remote or a Background notification, will define where it should go. For the first two options, local and background, it will prioritize the Apple Watch. Local Notifications on the other hand will prioritize depending on the source. Check the following image to see the different paths:

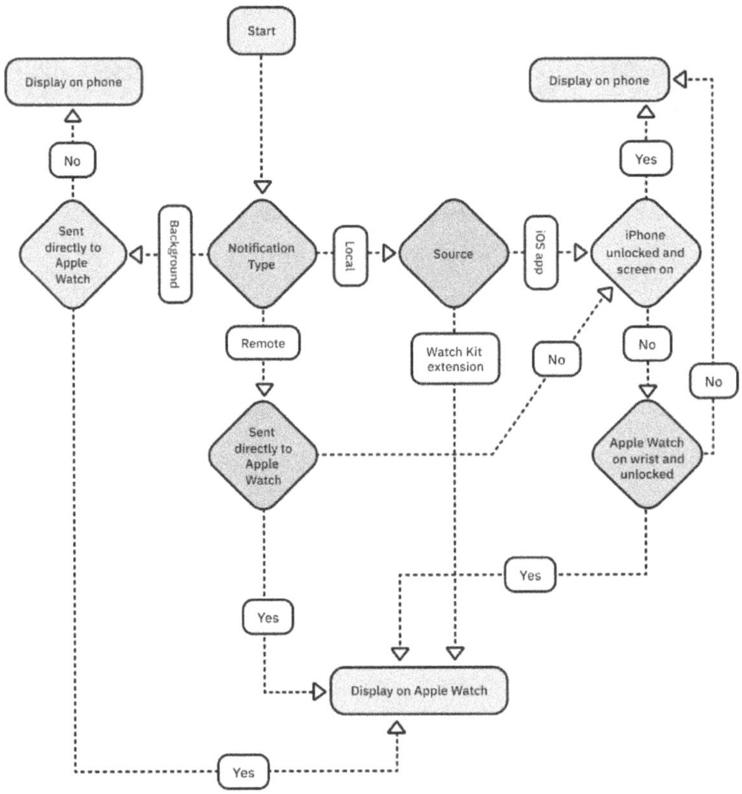

You'll notice two locations in the diagram where it asks if Apple sent the notification directly to the watch. In watchOS 6 and later, the Apple Watch is a valid target for remote and background notifications. The Apple Watch extension receives a unique device token when registering for remote notifications, just like in iOS.

Short Looks

When the Apple Watch receives a notification, it notifies the user via a subtle vibration. If the user views the notification by raising their wrist, the Apple Watch shows an abbreviated version called a **short look**. If the user views the notification for more than a split second, the Apple Watch will offer a more detailed version, or **long look**.

The short look notification is a quick summary for the user. Short looks show the app's icon and name, as well as the optional notification title, in a predefined layout:

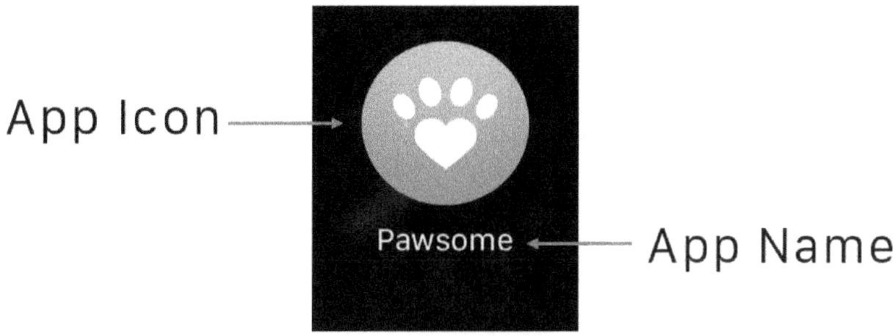

The optional notification title is a short blurb about the notification, such as "New Bill", "Reminder" or "Score Alert", and is added to the `alert` key's value. This lets the user decide whether to stick around for the long look interface.

Long Looks

The long look is a scrolling interface you can customize, with a default static interface or an optional dynamically-created interface. Unlike the short look interface, the long look offers significant customization.

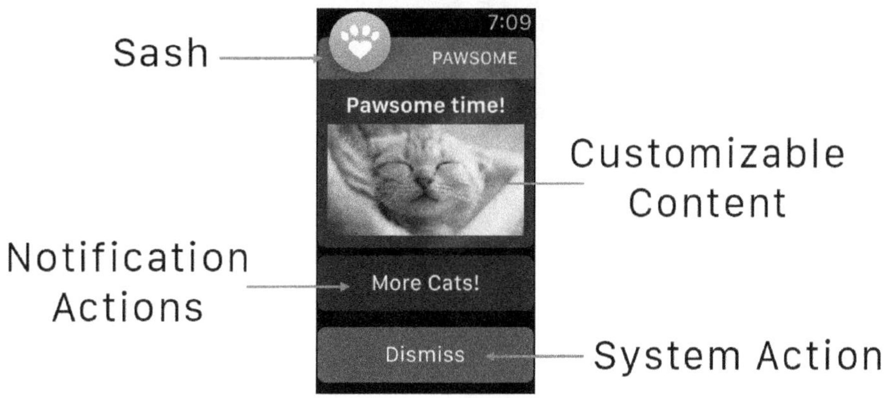

The **sash** is the horizontal bar at the top. It's translucent by default, but you can set it to any color and opacity value.

You can customize the content area by implementing a SwiftUI `View`, which you'll learn about later.

While you can implement several `UNNotificationAction` items, remember that more than a few will require quite a bit of scrolling on the user's part, leading to a poor user experience.

The system-provided Dismiss button is always present at the bottom of the interface. Tapping Dismiss hides the notification without informing the Apple Watch extension.

Now that you know about the short and long look notifications, it's time to put the theory into practice.

Testing Local Notifications

Pawsome is for all cat lovers who procrastinate during the day by looking at cute cat pictures. The Pawsome app will make this easier by interrupting you throughout the day with cute cat pictures that are certain to trigger a smile... unless you're a dog person!

Getting Started

Open the Pawsome starter project in Xcode. Then build and run the **Pawsome WatchKit App** scheme. You'll see a collection of cute kitty cats that you can easily browse:

Testing Notifications With the Simulator

When you make a new WatchKit app in Xcode, it will generate a notification run scheme used for testing the look and feel of your notifications. Switch to the **Pawsome WatchKit App (Notification)** scheme and rerun the project. This time, instead of seeing those adorable cats, you'll see a pretty boring notification:

It's not the *purrrtiest*, but you'll soon fix that.

Take a look at **LocalNotifications.swift**, and you'll see the code that creates and schedules your local notifications. There's nothing specific to watchOS, which is why I provided that file for you. At the top of the class, you'll find `categoryIdentifier`. When a notification triggers, that's the identifier you'll use.

Open **PawsomeApp.swift**. You'll see the following line, which Xcode adds if you say you want to include a notification when you create your project:

```
WKNotificationScene(
  controller: NotificationController.self,
  category: "myCategory"
)
```

Calling `WKNotificationScene` is how you tell the Apple Watch what view to display for each category identified in your payload. Replace the category with the one from `LocalNotifications`:

```
WKNotificationScene(
  controller: NotificationController.self,
  category: LocalNotifications.categoryIdentifier
)
```

Build and run the app. You'll see this notification:

What happened? The `NotificationView` wasn't updated, so why the change?

If you look at the **Run** step of the **Pawsome WatchKit App (Notification)** scheme, you'll see the notification payload is set to a file in your project, called **PushNotificationPayload.apns**:

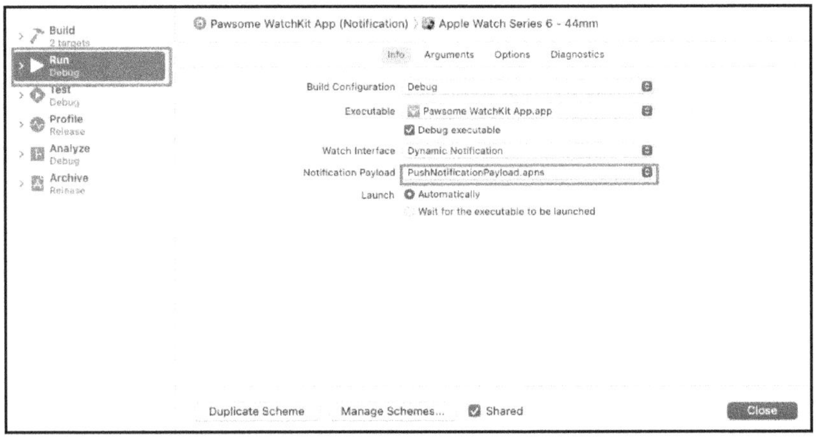

Take a look at **PushNotificationPayload.apns**. If you've worked with push notifications at all, this should look familiar to you. The **category** sent with the notification is set to **myCategory**. However, you updated **PawsomeApp.swift** to respond to a different category name. When the category sent to the app doesn't match something you've registered for, it configures a default display.

Change **myCategory** to **Pawsome**, which is the value of `LocalNotifications.categoryIdentifier`.

Run the app again. This time you'll see:

Where did the "More Cats!" button come from? **PawsomeApp.swift** creates an instance of `LocalNotifications`, which creates a default action button in its initializer.

Since the category in the JSON matches what you specified in `WKNotificationScene(controller:category:)`, watchOS created an instance of `NotificationController` and used that to display the notification. Look closely, and you'll notice the title and body are missing from the displayed view. Time to fix that!

Custom Long Look Notification

Edit **NotificationController.swift**, and you'll see `body` returns an instance of `NotificationView`. The *controller* is where you receive and parse the notification. The *view* is then where you use the data gathered by the controller.

Switch over to **NotificationView.swift** to make the notification appear the way you want. Replace the entire contents of the default file with:

```
import SwiftUI

struct NotificationView: View {
  // 1
  let message: String
  let image: Image

  // 2
  var body: some View {
    ScrollView {
      Text(message)
        .font(.headline)

      image
        .resizable()
```

```
        .scaledToFit()
      }
    }
  }

  struct NotificationView_Previews: PreviewProvider {
    static var previews: some View {
      // 3
      NotificationView(
        message: "Awww",
        image: Image("cat\(Int.random(in: 1...20))")
      )
    }
  }
```

The code is pretty straight-forward:

1. You need to provide a message and an image for the view to display.
2. The body simply displays those two properties in a scrolling list.
3. For the preview, a random image is chosen from the asset catalog for the previews.

Now that you've created a view to display when a notification arrives, it's time to use it. Head back to **NotificationController.swift** and replace the contents of the class with:

```
// 1
var image: Image!
var message: String!

// 2
override var body: NotificationView {
  return NotificationView(message: message, image: image)
}

// 3
override func didReceive(_ notification: UNNotification) {
  let content = notification.request.content
  message = content.body

  let num = Int.random(in: 1...20)
  image = Image("cat\(num)")
}
```

Like all good code, the controller is short and sweet. It only has a few steps:

1. You store the title and image so you can send them to the view.
2. Then you call the initializer for the view you're going to display, passing in the appropriate parameters.
3. You pull out the details from the payload body, which you then store in the class' properties.

Build and run again, trying to limit the immense feelings of joy caused by the display:

You probably want to display a specific cat, not a random one. Replace the last two lines of `didReceive(_:)` with:

```
let validRange = 1...20
if let imageNumber = content.userInfo["imageNumber"] as? Int,
  validRange ~= imageNumber {
  image = Image("cat\(imageNumber)")
} else {
  let num = Int.random(in: validRange)
  image = Image("cat\(num)")
}
```

The asset catalog provided with the starter project has images numbered from one to twenty. If the payload includes an image number in that range, you display the specified cat photo. If not, you provide a random image.

> **Note**: Since the view will always be generated, you need to ensure that valid data is always available, even if it means presenting a default set of data.

Add the following line right before the final closing } character in **PushNotificationPayload.apns**:

```
, "imageNumber": 5
```

Build and run again. You'll see **cat5** from the asset catalog.

Receiving Remote Push Notifications

Most apps use push notifications, not local notifications. You're probably wondering why I spent all that time on something that's used less frequently. Well, the answer is that Apple made push notifications much easier on watchOS than they are on iOS.

In iOS, you have to create an extension to modify the incoming payload and yet another extension if you want a custom interface. Worse yet, you can't natively perform the custom interface with SwiftUI as of iOS 16. In watchOS, push notifications work exactly like local notifications!

Everything you learned about using `WKUserNotificationHostingController` to parse the payload and return a custom SwiftUI `View` works the same when you're developing push notifications.

Create a WKExtensionDelegate

In iOS, you register for push notifications using `AppDelegate`. That class doesn't exist on watchOS. Instead, you use `WKExtensionDelegate`. Create a new Swift file called **ExtensionDelegate.swift** and paste:

```
import WatchKit
import UserNotifications

// 1
```

```
final class ExtensionDelegate: NSObject, WKExtensionDelegate {
  // 2
  func didRegisterForRemoteNotifications(withDeviceToken
deviceToken: Data) {
    print(deviceToken.reduce("") { $0 + String(format: "%02x",
$1) })
  }

  // 3
  func applicationDidFinishLaunching() {
    Task {
      do {
        let success = try await UNUserNotificationCenter
          .current()
          .requestAuthorization(options:
[.badge, .sound, .alert])

        guard success else { return }

        // 4
        await MainActor.run {
          WKExtension.shared().registerForRemoteNotifications()
        }
      } catch {
        print(error.localizedDescription)
      }
    }
  }
}
```

Here's a code breakdown:

1. You declare a class that implements `WKExtensionDelegate`. Since that protocol is based on `NSObjectProtocol` you also need to derive from `NSObject`.
2. Just like in iOS, you grab the `deviceToken` whenever registration happens. A production app would, of course, store and use the token, not just print it.
3. Surprisingly not named `extensionDidFinishLaunching`. You do the standard dance in this method to request permission to use push notifications.
4. If permissions are granted, you use the `WKExtension` singleton to register for push notifications, which call `didRegisterForRemoteNotifications(withDeviceToken:)` if successful.

To tell watchOS it should use your `ExtensionDelegate`, add the following two lines to the top of the `struct` in **PawsomeApp.swift**:

```
@WKExtensionDelegateAdaptor(ExtensionDelegate.self)
private var extensionDelegate
```

The MVC of Push Notifications

Instead of making you copy and paste a ton of code, I've provided a **Remote Notifications** group in the starter project, which contains the relevant files for a push notification.

Generally, you'll want to use some type of model to represent the data that will pass between your `WKUserNotificationHostingController` and `View`. While you could use individual properties, as in the preceding examples for local notifications, it's better to use a real model, such as the one provided in **RemoteNotificationModel.swift**.

Look at **RemoteNotificationView.swift**, and you'll see it's just a simple setup that shows a small number of details by default. If you tap the toggle, it displays more details. Remember, unlike the iPhone, the Apple Watch has limited display space. You'll need to think differently about how you present notification data to the user.

Next, open **RemoteNotificationController.swift**. Even though you're working with a remote push notification, you'll see everything works the same as when you implemented local notifications. Pay special attention to the `guard` statement.

In an ideal world, the payload provided to your app would always be 100% perfect. However, we don't live in an ideal world, so it's important to always validate the input. If anything goes wrong, you *still* have to provide a model for the notification to display. Don't let your app crash because of bad data!

Adding the Capability

Xcode will perform magic if you add the **Push Notifications** capability. In the Project navigator (**Command-1**), select the project name, **Pawsome**. Then select the **Pawsome Watch App** target.

On the **Signing & Capabilities** tab, add the **Push Notifications** capability. If you try to add a capability and nothing seems to show, that generally means you haven't chosen the correct target.

> **Note**: Xcode does not generate a valid identifier for watchOS push notifications!

Years ago, Apple finally automated almost everything around certificate and identifier generation. Unfortunately, for watchOS push notifications, it broke things.

The solution, while annoying to have to deal with, is quite simple. Go into your team's Certificates, Identifiers & Profiles (https://apple.co/31pwmKV) page on the Apple Developer Portal and manually create an identifier for your watchOS app. Use the app identifier **com.yourcompany.Pawsome.watchkitapp** and add Push Notification support.

> **Note**: Replace **yourcompany** in the app identifier with your team's name.

Add a Scheme

Edit the current scheme via your preferred method. I like to press the **Command+<** keyboard shortcut, or you can click on the current scheme and then click **Edit Scheme...**.

The default project Xcode created includes a notification scheme you used to test the local notifications. You'll need another scheme to test the remote notification because the payload is a different file. You could, of course, just change the file on the existing scheme if you wanted to.

> **Note**: If your app supports more than one notification, you can add multiple APNS files and multiple schemes to make it easy to test each one.

Follow these steps to configure a new scheme:

1. With the notification scheme still chosen, press **Duplicate Scheme** at the bottom of the dialog window.
2. Choose a name for the new scheme, such as **Push Notification**.
3. Click **Run** on the left side of the dialog window.
4. Select **RemotePush.apns** as the notification payload to use.

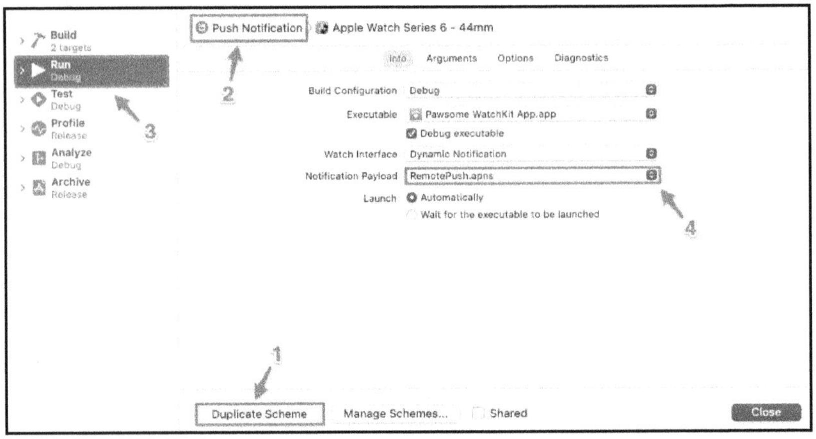

The starter project already includes an .apns file. In your own projects you'll have to add a new one. You'll find **RemotePush.apns** in **Remote Notifications**. It contains a simple example remote push notification payload:

```
{
  "aps": {
    "alert": {
      "body": "Lorem ipsum dolor sit amet, consectetur...",
      "title": "Lorem Ipsum",
    },
    "category": "lorem"
  },

  "date": "2021-04-01T12:00:00Z"
}
```

Remember that watchOS has no way of associating a payload to a controller if you don't link them. Go back into **PawsomeApp.swift** and add the following statement:

```
WKNotificationScene(
  controller: RemoteNotificationController.self,
  category: RemoteNotificationController.categoryIdentifier
)
```

Build and run to take a look at how your remote notification would look on watchOS!

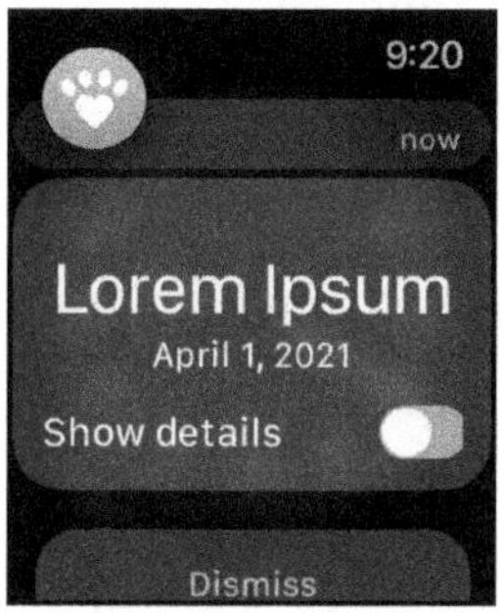

Interactive Notifications

Tap **Show details**. Did something unexpected happen? An average user would expect to see details. Instead, you were taken into the app and shown a cat picture. Surprisingly, that's by design.

By default, push notifications are not interactive. As far as the Apple Watch knows, anything that's not one of the action buttons is just an image on the screen.

Adding an action button wouldn't make sense to show more details. Instead, add the following line to **RemoteNotificationController**:

```
override class var isInteractive: Bool { true }
```

Build and run again. This time, when you tap the toggle, the details appear and disappear as you'd expect them to:

The `isInteractive` type property of `WKUserNotificationHostingController` specifies whether the notification should accept user input. The default value is `false`, meaning you can only interact with buttons. By changing the value to `true`, you tell watchOS the notification should accept user input.

You solved one problem but might have introduced another. Tapping no longer opens the app. If the user taps the app icon or anywhere on the sash, the app will still open.

Great work! Now you know how to add custom notification interfaces to your Watch apps. The rest is up to you! With the power of SwiftUI you are free to put any sort of view on the screen you can imagine, just like on iOS.

APNs Request

A key difference between iOS notifications and watchOS notifications is that you *must* include the **apns-push-type** HTTP header for the Apple Watch to receive a notification.

Apple's Sending Notification Requests to APNs (https://apple.co/3sNr7U4) documents the HTTP headers that you might need to send as part of your POST to APNs.

Key Points

- How Local & Remote Notifications work with Apple Watch.
- Short & Long looks and how to customize them.
- Testing Push Notifications on Apple Watch
- Ensure your server includes the **apns-push-type** HTTP header.

Where to Go From Here?

In this chapter, you tested Watch notifications, learned about short look and long look interfaces and how they differ. Most impressively, you built a custom, dynamically updating, long look local notification for the Apple Watch.

For more details on creating schemes and JSON payloads, as well as testing directly on the watch, please see Testing Custom Notifications (https://apple.co/3tTDE5F) in Apple's developer documentation.

15 Conclusion

Congratulations for completing Push Notifications by Tutorials!

We hope you're excited about the knowledge that you've gained throughout this book, learning how to create highly professional push notifications with the latest features and abilities.

As you've learned in this book, push notifications are conceptually simple. But what eventually makes an app stand out in the crowd comes down to all of the advanced features and abilities you've mastered in this book: rich notifications with a custom UI, location and time-based notifications, custom actions, grouped notifications and much more!

You've also briefly touched on how to create your very own server and what are the various customization options in your disposal when building and delivering your own payload.

We've spent an enormous amount of time, love and effort to makes this book the best and most accessible resource for iOS push notifications. If you have any questions, comments or suggestions, please stop by our forums at https://forums.raywenderlich.com.

Thank you, again, for purchasing this book. Your continued support is what makes the books, tutorials, videos and other things we do at raywenderlich.com possible. We truly appreciate it!

– Scott and Marin